# Technostress

# TECHNO STRESS

## The Human Cost of the Computer Revolution

## Craig Brod

Addison-Wesley Publishing Company
Reading, Massachusetts   Menlo Park, California
London   Amsterdam   Don Mills, Ontario   Sydney

**Library of Congress Cataloging in Publication Data**

Brod, Craig.
   Technostress: the human cost of the computer revolution.

   Bibliography: p.
   Includes index.
   1. Electronic digital computers—Psychological aspects.
2. Stress (Psychology)   I. Title.
QA76.9.P75B76   1984      001.64      83–25866
ISBN 0–201–11211–6

Jacket design by Marshall Henrichs. Jacket photograph by Thomas Porett/Photo Researchers. Text design by Lori Snell. Set in 11-point Century Expanded by Datapage Division, Western Publishing Company.

ISBN 0–201–11211–6

ABCDEFGHIJ-DO-87654

First printing, January 1984

*To those among us who had the courage to expose the truth of their altered lives.*

# Contents

*ix*  Acknowledgments

*xi*  Preface

**ONE**
*1*  Groundswell

**TWO**
*25*  The Mental Sweatshop

**THREE**
*61*  Of Managers and Micros

**FOUR**
*83*  Robot/Human—Human/Robot

**FIVE**
*101*  An End to Romance

**SIX**
*121*  Childhood Lost

**SEVEN**
*141*  Video Kids

**EIGHT**

*169*  Managing Electronic Space

**NINE**

*191*  Closing the Generation Gap

**TEN**

*211*  Salvaging Souls

*221*  Postscript

*225*  Bibliography

*237*  Index

# Acknowledgments

I WOULD LIKE to express my profound thanks to the many people who have given their help and support during the time I worked on this book. It is impossible for me to mention all of them by name. However, I am especially grateful to:

Doe Coover and Cyrisse Jaffee, my editors at Addison-Wesley, who paid untiring attention to the manuscript and to my development as a writer.

Doug Stewart, a skillful text editor whose writing and editorial skills helped the manuscript move far beyond its original limits. Without Doug the book would have been unduly delayed.

Gale Grossman, who performed valuable research by conducting interviews and retrieving little-known but important data on adaptation to computers. She served as an important commentator on my own clinical perceptions.

Hy Janov, in loving memory, and Cyril Brod, my grandfathers, who helped me trust my own perceptions of the world and to finance my education. They made it possible for me to grow up thinking carefully.

Sandra Brod, my sister, for her encouragement and emotional support. She often provided solace in moments of anxiety and confusion.

Mary Tondorf-Dick, whose suggestions upon reading the original manuscript helped expand the scope of the work.

Rebecca Heinz and Marcy McGaugh, who did a superb job transcribing interviews and converting handwritten parts of the manuscript to typed copy. They often produced despite the pressure of tight deadlines.

Graduate students in Psychology at Antioch University, San Francisco, who helped conduct interviews and call my attention to significant details.

# Preface

MANY PEOPLE SPEAK in the following pages. Their
conversations, disclosed to me during three years of in-
depth interviews, concern the anxiety and fear people experience when attempting to master the computer. They
reveal unsettling dreams, endless hours of tension, and
often disappointment—all in learning to manage and use
the new technology effectively. Most important, the words
of these people reveal the impact the computer has had on
their ability to sustain personal relationships.

This is the first book to address the current struggle
of individuals to adapt to computer technology. It is also
a chronicle of the disease that results when the delicate
balance between people and computers is violated. I call
that disease technostress.

Many experiences led to my discovery of technostress. The one that triggered my thinking occurred when
a seasoned computer programmer who worked at a large
urban bank was referred to me for therapy. During a
psychotherapy session he presented general complaints of
feeling down and depleted. He also complained of marital
problems. His wife, he stated jokingly, made a horrible
peripheral—jargon for a computer accessory.

Although his symptoms clearly suggested depression, I found myself asking detailed questions about his
work life. He shared with me the pressures of his work,
the demands on his brain, how he lost himself in a project
—"into the vortex," as he aptly put it. I perceived him as
a person who was addicted to work, which only masked his
depression. However, there remained a particular cogni-

tive pattern that I couldn't explain. In the course of several months he helped me to understand how the nature of his work had influenced him. Slowly we began to understand that it was not his personality type or his past that was causing his symptoms. The problem was inherent in the work itself.

In order to pursue this phenomenon further I decided to interview people in organizational contexts on all levels and in all phases of computer adaptation. This proved difficult, since managers, generally, did not know how to implement new technologies, and they were afraid to have their ignorance exposed. Also, computer companies, which made great promises to employers who purchased their technology, did not want anything uncovered that might enhance negative attitudes toward their machines. Nevertheless, those who worked with computers—from clerical workers to CEOs to computer programmers—consistently revealed to me the striking effects that computers were having on their professional and personal lives. Not only were they contending with easily recognizable stress reactions such as headaches and fatigue, they were beginning to internalize the standards by which the computer works: accelerated time, a desire for perfection, yes-no patterns of thinking. These internalized standards combined to reduce the ability of the person to perform creatively or to relate to others in a loving way.

After discovering technostress in adults, I wondered if children, who have become some of our most avid computer users, were likewise affected. Fresh with general themes that had been gleaned from adults—such as the orientation to time, perceptual modes, styles of communication, damaged interpersonal relationships—I began to interview children from five to sixteen years old. (I tried to balance male and female interviews, but this was difficult because boys who use computers tend to outnumber girls substantially.) I also interviewed many adolescents, because that stage is acknowledged as a critical period in human development. Technostress would have a greater impact on the personality over a longer period if it existed there. Unfortunately, I found widespread symptoms of technostress among young people. More machinelike than childlike, these children seek isolation from family members, view others as highly inefficient, and experience traditional learning activities like reading as painfully slow. They have been socialized by the computer.

The societal implications of technostress cannot be ignored. We are in danger of moving farther and farther away from the bright and productive people we hope to be. Even as we recognize intimate relationships—man-woman and parent-child—as the most valuable forum for exploring our own humanity and individuality, we are creating serious obstacles to that which we most cherish. In its most severe stages, technostress may be threatening our survival as a species.

This book is an opportunity for people to test the discovery of technostress against their own experiences and to use the suggested solutions I offer to eliminate or mediate the negative effects of a technocentered culture. I have included strategies for managers, teachers, psychologists, couples, and parents. It is my belief that an awareness of technostress and its remedies will be our best hope for the future.

Specialization, ironically, was the beginning of the road to extinction. This was the essential theme that time had dramatized upon the giant stage.

Loren Eiseley

# ONE

## Groundswell

"There are some people who still think a
computer is a black box that processes data."

*Linda*
Systems analyst

2    AMERICAN SOCIETY is in love with the computer. As a companion in our daily lives, it is rapidly becoming ubiquitous. The growth and proliferation of computers in our society is staggering: in 1980, twenty-four companies sold 724,000 personal computers. By 1983, one single company —Apple—had sold over a million. Experts estimate that by 1988 nearly sixty percent of the American work force will be linked to electronic work stations. There are now more than 350,000 computers in the nation's schools, as opposed to half the number only two years ago. At any given moment on Wall Street there are five times as many computers communicating with each other as people. In offices, factories, schools, libraries, banks, and homes all across the country, the computer has changed the way we live.

The American people have embraced the computer revolution with unquestioning confidence. With so many environmental frontiers exhausted, the seemingly unlimited capability and versatility of the computer is, in effect, a bold new frontier for us to explore and conquer. We have always sought to challenge the limits of the natural world; computer technology satisfies our traditional notion of progress—bigger is better—by enabling us to store, process, and access vast amounts of information. Having conquered the broad, open spaces of the world around us, we have begun to develop a new notion of progress: the mastery of the microworld.

Although we may admit that it is "just a machine," our fascination with the computer echoes our fascination with our own power to achieve; we declare the computer to be an extension of the human brain—yet better, faster, without limits. It has captured our hearts because it taps our deepest desires. Computer technology promises to perform our tasks effortlessly, efficiently, and speedily. Responsive and dependable, the computer remembers everything. From genetic engineering to the microchip, we are thrilled by our abilities to tackle the most basic units of matter.

As we rush headlong into an increasingly computer-ized society, a new faith is developing. Its basic tenet is: Computer technology is the harbinger of a brighter and more secure future. Those who preach the faith include educators who believe computers will enable us to teach and learn more effectively; researchers in artificial intelli-gence who talk excitedly about machines that "think"; politicians who herald the arrival of the high-tech industry as economic and political salvation; and, of course, com-puter companies that promote a glowing image of a smoothly functioning universe. The media have seized that image with gusto, generating books, articles, and stories about the miraculous and utopian nature of this brand-new cultural superstar.

But love being blind, our devotion to the new machine prevents us from seeing the possible consequences of spending long hours—in work and at play—with a ma-chine. It inhibits us from asking the most significant questions about the changes in ourselves and our children —physical, psychological, and social—resulting from our relentless pursuit of a technocentered culture. It is essen-tial that we examine the impact of the computer on our lives, our jobs, our schools. We all know, for example, that the automobile has enabled us to travel faster; yet we blithely pay a high price for this technological advance— fifty thousand annual traffic fatalities, railroads and public transit systems in decay, city centers divided and subdi-vided by freeways, and air quality warnings on the morn-ing news. With the advent of computerized technology, we must take heed of its perils as well as its merits. Certainly,

3

the computer helps many of us to be more productive; but its magic is not entirely benign. The computer revolution—the massive upheaval and restructuring of society by technology—should be what we consciously choose to make of it. If we rush to embrace it as a cure-all, we will lose our chance to make the kinds of choices that will genuinely improve our quality of life. And if we don't choose wisely, we will regret our hastiness—if, that is, we have retained enough perspective to notice what we have sacrificed.

4

In order to begin to ask and to answer vital questions about the influence of computers, we must carefully examine the creed of the computer faithful, to separate hype from reality, fact from fiction. Having done this, we can begin to integrate the technology in our lives without risking our collective well-being.

Computers are touted as the most significant advance in the history of civilization. But the high esteem in which they are held is based on a negative sell unprecedented in history. Ironically, we are motivated by fear to accept what is supposed to bring security and hope. Workers and managers fear obsolescence if they are not at the technological forefront. Parents, concerned about the demands of future educators and employers, feel compelled to make sure their children are computer-literate at an early age. Those who do not join in the revolution will, we are told, become relics of a backward culture.

With a negative sell has come a national sell. President Reagan told the American people that high technology will be the solution to our troubles at home and abroad. It will curb unemployment and revitalize our economy, and return America to its rightful rank in the world. Our national ego, sorely bruised in recent years, will be rejuvenated. Despite the fact that our particular brand of progress has often been made at a considerable cost, we continue to view it as a stellar American virtue. Anyone who hesitates in this endeavor, therefore, is not only old-fashioned, but un-American. The cherished dream of every American worker—successful entrepreneurship

—has been rekindled by the phenomenal growth of small computer companies. And yet the troubled state of the microcomputer industry, and the demise in 1983 of the Osborne Computer Corporation, once a leader in portable computers, are signals that the bubble has already burst. With one hundred fifty different personal computer manufacturers battling for their share of the market, that entrepreneurial dream, glamorized by the success of Apple, Intel, and others, is already history. Already, economists are warning that the computer industry is subject to the same boom-bust cycles that have plagued other American industries.

5

Being computer-literate today will not guarantee you a more interesting or secure job—it may not provide you with a job at all. Economists are not sure what the long-lasting effects of the growth of the computer industry will be, measured against the loss of jobs due to automation. In a sluggish economy, there is no need for the displaced to reenter the labor force. Not every jobless welder can be retrained and employed as a computer repair person.

A contradiction, in fact, is developing within the work force. On the one hand, the educational level of workers as a whole is increasing. On the other, the computer in many situations is generating very little interesting work, except for executives or research-and-development workers. Most people attached to a computer only process data. What is emerging is a two-class work force: one class is told what to do by the computer; the other tells the computer what to do. The former consists of those who, bored and edgy, spend their days in front of the screen, obeying commands. The latter struggle with machinery deadlines and the intellectual demands of producing more and more programs, feeling just as disgruntled as their subordinates. "If I died," remarks one, "the machine would just keep plugging away."

Middle managers find their jobs redefined or phased out as more functions are computerized, requiring less supervisory personnel. Clerical positions may be increas-

ing—for jobs whose routine aspects are amplified and multiplied. In the not too distant future, even those clerical jobs may disappear; if a bank has to pay more for human tellers than for automated teller machines, for instance, the tellers may soon find themselves joining the ranks of the unemployed. Blue-collar workers are similarly threatened by computerization: some factories in Europe operate with a fraction of the laborers they once used. The computer industry added only slightly more than 200,000 jobs in 1982, and didn't generate the accompanying increase in support industries—unlike the growth of previous industries, such as automobiles, which depended on increased production of steel, glass, rubber, and aluminum. The computer industry is not immune to the use of cheap foreign labor that has so undercut American workers: in 1982 Atari, a manufacturer of computer games owned by Warner Communications, fired twelve hundred workers in the Silicon Valley and moved part of its operations to Asia.

Moreover, the computer-literate children of today may be baffled by the technology ten years from now, or find that their knowledge of programming has been rendered unnecessary by more sophisticated machines. We may be repeating our experience of the 1960s, when, in the aftermath of Sputnik, we raced to train teachers and aerospace engineers. A decade later, both professions suffered from shifts in the nation's needs. Our response to the challenge of Japanese and German technical sophistication is no different. But in the face of voice-activation, touch control, and machines without keyboards, the push to merge children and computers may well be creating a generation that is unmotivated, resentful, overburdened, and unemployed.

One of the most seductive features of the computer is its incredible speed. Our expectation is that computer technology, with its split-second accuracy, will save time, make our work easier, and create more leisure time. But computers are anything but mere replacements for pen, paper, and typewriter. By offering us so much power, speed, and accuracy, they are expanding at a breathless pace our concept of what we can—and should—do. Equipped with a portable business computer, Sam Armacost, the forty-four-year-old chief executive of the Bank of America, stays in touch with a dozen other top executives of the bank. At Armacost's "suggestion," the other senior executives have been trained to run their systems at the office and home. They can "talk" to one another at any time, day or night. Do these executives really find that being constantly on-line has afforded them more free time?

7

The instruction manual for WordStar, a popular word-processing program, is filled with credibility-stretching cartoons showing relaxed and happy computer operators. "Thanks to WordStar," exults one caption, "I have time for a cup of coffee, too!" But although time may be saved on a particular task, work as a whole tends to proliferate. If, for example, typists can type twice as many letters in a day as they could before, their employers will expect them to double their output. Telephone operators won't suddenly find more time during the workday for socializing but will be expected to work at a more furious pace. As our idea of what we can accomplish in a day is reduced to a matter of hours, and then a matter of minutes, our sense of time is profoundly altered and compressed.

Outside the office, personal computers are often promoted as an indispensable adjunct to daily life. Aside from games and word processing, the home computer turns out to be quite dispensable after all. According to an eight-page magazine foldout put out by Apple, a personal computer can teach a dog to heel, analyze the Rorschach ink-blot test, teach music writing, and help its user meditate. While there may be some Apple owners who have tried these applications, it is generally more effective to pursue these activities in the traditional manner.

We often don't have a specific reason for buying a microcomputer, other than a vague fear of being left behind. Computer store managers have reported in surveys that first-time buyers have returned to the store after a few days to ask for ideas on how to use their new acquisitions. Creating a need for a product, while profitable, can be dangerous; the study of cultures in transition has shown that such manipulation may cause revolt. Some refuse to use the computer altogether, abandoning the word processor for the electric or even manual typewriter. Others subtly resist by sabotaging the technology or finding excuses for not learning how to use it. Amidst the cries of enthusiasm there is an underlying current of conflict and anger.

In *The Third Wave*, Alvin Toffler presents a sanguine view of the impact of the computer. He claims that with the communications revolution, mankind will increasingly "own the technology of consciousness." Toffler, who recognizes that there are powerful forces at work altering our social character, admits that his speculations may be shaky, but remains optimistic:

> If our assumptions are even partially correct, individuals will vary more vividly tomorrow than they do today. More of them are likely to . . . evince greater individuality . . . to crave balance in their lives—balance between work and play, between production and consumption, between headwork and handwork, between abstract and concrete, between objectivity and subjectivity. And they will see and project themselves in far more complex terms than any previous people. As the Third Wave civilization matures we will create not a utopian man or woman . . . but merely, and proudly, one hopes, a race—and a civilization—that deserves to be called human.

For a writer (like Toffler), a home computer and a word-processing program can seem like a wonderful thing. But for the hospital bureaucrat buried in computer printouts, or the insurance company employee who finds her keystrokes tallied automatically, the computer is primarily a source of stress. Even for those who try to use computers creatively—an architect who designs buildings with a stylus and video-display terminal (VDT), for example, or the aeronautical engineer who runs flight simulations electronically—the computer provides neither variety nor balance. In fact, it is cutting us off more and more from the outside world. For thousands of years we have learned by observing the details of the cultures we live in. Now, suddenly, we find ourselves doing much of our work and play essentially by remote control. Where once a boy and his father may have worked side by side to build a table, learning about the properties of wood, hammer, and nails, now they sit in front of a screen handling abstract data. As we learn more and more directly from the computer and less from our own experiences, we may be losing the important tactile dimension that is so crucial to the development of true intelligence. Designers, architects, and engineers may be able to create clothes, cars, or buildings that function well, but they will lose the individuality and eccentricity that inspires breakthroughs. They will also move further and further away from the human dimension that makes their work aesthetic.

9

As a society, we are intrigued by the notion of a machine with a mind, of the potential possibilities of "artificial intelligence." Since the computer's abilities are seen as boundless, we have somehow assumed that it will stretch our mental capacities by enabling us to learn and think faster and further. The speed with which it can perform math, from simple addition to complex algebra, seems both magical and practical. But as we become increasingly dependent on calculators and VisiCalc—at the office, in the grocery store, or in the classroom—we may be neglecting to teach the fundamentals that allow for true comprehension, and the ability to solve problems creatively and patiently.

At St. Anne's School in Brooklyn, New York, ninth-graders are "taught" Einstein's theory of relativity using a computer program designed by William Everdell. Students tell the computer their weight at rest, then punch in a speed in miles per hour. The computer might display the following message: "Sorry, you have gained. You now weigh 165.0000002 pounds." Everdell comments, "Now everybody seems to know what the special theory of relativity is all about." In fact, what the students know is that as you approach the speed of light, you gain weight. This may be a valuable lesson, and fun to do, but it hardly offers a solid understanding of Einstein's theory. Yet students, parents, and even teachers believe that because they handle more information faster, they are getting smarter.

The intimate proximity of the computer in our lives in general, and the model of "thinking machines" in particular, are causing many of us to confuse machine operations and human thought. A new cognitive science is emerging at whose center is a theory of mind based on the notion that the human brain operates like a computer. Mental states are compared to computer states, and mental processes to computational processes. Researchers are delving into the chemical and electrical bases of emotion and learning, and some scientists go so far as to make the case that human emotions may actually be nothing more than a complex set of decision routines. M. Toda, a well-known Japanese psychologist, describes emotions as "vexing appendages" and goes on to say:

> Emotions are decision-making programs developed through evolution . . . They may have first emerged for the purpose of the survival of the species, but those that particularly enrich human experience seem to be directed toward increasing the level of rationality of human groups. Human beings, however, have greatly enlarged their information-processing capacity, which has given rise to an analytical nonemotional way of making decisions.

Many neurophysiologists, such as Karl Pribram at Stanford University, have had to revise this equating of the human brain and the computer. The human brain is, in fact, too unique, complex, and intricate to be compared to the relatively simple and logical structure of the computer. If the memory that is stored in one computer chip is damaged, for example, the entire system may be significantly changed or destroyed. However, since information content is distributed throughout the human brain, it will continue to function despite minor damage.

11

Even the computer industry itself once recognized that the human brain and the computer are not identical models. Almost thirty years ago, a top executive at IBM handed his staff a dictum that forbade, on pain of being fired, anthropomorphizing the computer. He was alarmed at the growing tendency of staffers to speak of the computer's information storage and retrieval system as a memory. While the computer successfully simulates one aspect of human memory, it otherwise resembles it only superficially because humans recall experience and emotion as well as data.

The push to examine the mind using machine metaphors can be attributed, in part, to the popular tendency to view the computer as the ideal accompaniment to our next evolutionary step forward. Carl Sagan, in *The Dragons of Eden,* asserts: "the next major structural development in human intelligence is likely to be a partnership between intelligent humans and intelligent machines." In *The Electronic Cottage,* Joseph Deaken joyfully predicts: "this logical brain tool we have constructed is literally going to wake up and be a mover and shaker." But some experts doubt that machines can ever be characterized as "thinking," and although computers may indeed affect our evolution as a species, they may prove to be less than desirable partners.

The computer industry has developed the term "user-friendly" to assure everyone that computers are easy to use, accommodating, nonthreatening, and comforting companions with which to tackle problems. But one owner of a computer store that specializes in word-processing systems notes, "Because computers have been advertised so heavily on TV, we're finding that many customers have sky-high expectations. Just look at some of the product names: Easy Writer, Magic Wand. We have to bring the customers down from the clouds a bit—make them aware of the learning curve they encounter when adapting to computers." The founders of Apple Computer, Inc., Steven Jobs and Stephen Wozniak, purposely used a homey name for their first product: Apple. Their newest personal computer, geared to the executive market, is called Lisa.

In reality, computers can be frustrating and confusing to use and profoundly impersonal. The logic of the system places limits on its flexibility. For example, it can't handle ambiguous instructions. Programs often take months to learn. Sometimes the manuals that are intended to teach the software are as impenetrable as the hardware itself. The introductory book for the IBM Personal Computer is so confusing that a guide for the guide had to be published. What starts out as a "friendly" experience may become a nerve-racking struggle to master the program. Anyone who has ever been baffled by programming instructions, or has had to wait at an airport, bank, or library while the machines were off-line, or has pressed the "help" button on the computer's keyboard to no avail, can tell you that computers are often not very friendly at all.

In advertisements for computers, the high-tech office is uncluttered and serene, while the traditional office is pictured as noisy and hectic. Indeed, the admittedly pressured (but often exciting and good-humored) traditional office milieu has been replaced by a new kind of environment: one in which humans are expected to perform in accordance with machines.

Placed abruptly in that setting, and reassured that the computer is merely a new (and easily digestible) addition to office equipment, most of us end up feeling incompetent, ill at ease, blaming ourselves for a lack of adaptability to systems that are actually difficult to comprehend. The high-tech industry has tried to allay our anxiety by claiming the computer is merely a tool to be used as we see fit. But in our naive acceptance of the computer we have failed to realize the new values, integral to a technocentered culture, that we are absorbing.

Tools have always set in motion great changes within human societies. Tools create us as much as we create them. The spear, for example, did much more than extend a hunter's reach; it changed the hunter's gait and use of his arms. It encouraged better eye-hand coordination; it led to social organizations for tracking, killing, and retrieving larger prey. It widened the gap between the unskilled and skilled hunter and made pooling of information more important as hunting excursions became more complex. There were other, less obvious effects: changes in the diets of hunting societies led to sharing of food and the formation of new social relationships. The value of craftsmanship increased. People began to plan ahead, storing weapons for reuse. All of these new tool-created demands, in turn, spurred greater development of the brain. Brain complexity led to new tools, and new tools made yet more complex brains advantageous to the survival of the species.

13

The modern human brain is roughly triple the size of an ape's. Its size and complexity do not merely enable us to learn skills; they have made such learning essential to survival. The human infant is helpless, its brain unorganized within an unknitted skull. An infant's brain resembles that of an ape, but it has several new areas in the cortex that enable advanced use of the hands, language comprehension, and improved memory. With its large association area, the advanced human brain makes complex language possible and distinguishes us as human.

As we have evolved from our primate ancestors we have had to impart more and more knowledge to our children—how to communicate, how to use society's tools, how to function within the community—thus prolonging infancy and childhood. We have moved away from the patterns of instinct. Whereas in the past an inappropriate diet or ungainly body type may have led to a species' demise, today it is the brain itself that holds the key to our survival. We are no longer struggling simply to adapt to natural conditions; our struggle is to adapt to the products we have created.

14

We can barely comprehend the true effects that our increasing involvement with computers (the newest and perhaps most influential tool-system) is having on our evolutionary and societal development. The spear's effects on our eye-hand coordination, for instance, are moderate compared to what the computer is beginning to do to our mental coordination. Eyes, muscles, and bones adapt slowly, but the human brain is prone to extremely rapid adaptation. It has enabled us to survive creatively in various environments. Since learning is now essential to survival in the modern world, the manner in which knowledge is transmitted from one generation to another—and what kind of knowledge is required by each generation—has a greater effect on our evolutionary course. If we continue to equate the simple logic of a machine with the complex workings of the human brain, we endanger our inherent ability to find creative solutions to the inevitably complex problems of the future.

The introduction of the computer is the most dramatic upheaval we have ever faced because of its potential to alter the human brain and because of the host of fundamental changes it has brought to our society. It has placed a machine as the central hero and metaphor of our time. *Time* magazine selected the computer as Man of the Year ("having the greatest influence for good or evil") for 1982. We idolize the computer's qualities: speed, efficiency, obedience, accuracy, rigidity, conformity. We're particularly obsessed with speed: fast food, instant information, quick cures. We demand "instant information on information itself," as the Xerox advertisement reads. Stockbrokers fret without split-second market news, complete and error-free. Grocery clerks groan when their cash register's laser fails to read an automatic pricing code.

Unwittingly, we are adopting as our own the computer's standards. We have come to expect from people the perfection, accuracy, and speed to which computers have made us accustomed. Busy following standardized procedures and ultralogical reasoning in order to interact with computers, we have begun to think of conversation as data transfer and memory as a search procedure. We already are beginning to speak like machines: "I need more data" or "I can't access that." The directory-assistance operator, the bank teller, the ticket agent, the librarian have all become computer operators with whom we "interface." As we grow more and more impatient with human imperfection and variation, we move further and further away from the very essence of our own humanity.

We are diminishing and altering our sense of self and of others, creating new barriers to what we long for: intimacy, continuity, and community. In fact, there's precious little room left for humor, empathy, joy, or love.

If we continue to internalize the machine model as well as its standards, we will transform ourselves into genuine extensions of the machine: we will redefine what is human. Ironically, the limit to technological progress is that while technology promises a qualitatively more advanced life, in reality the ultralogical nature of the machine, however beguiling, closes off more possibilities than it opens. And yet, because we are so convinced of the merits of the computer revolution, we are unwilling to pause and reflect on the very real human costs it is exacting.

Computers are affecting our personalities, behavior, and thus our relationships to our jobs and our families in discernible and alarming ways. Consider the following cases:

David, a psychiatrist, bought a personal computer to

keep track of patient billings. He quickly became an avid
user, buying new software packages and learning how to
write his own programs. Lately he has found his patients
are frustrating him. They are slow to respond to questions,
he thinks; they don't say things that are particularly interesting, and when they do their responses to his questions
are too ambiguous to be useful to their care. Recently,
David has been pushing his patients to get to the point.
Once he dozed off during a session.

16     Kenneth is a junior high school student. Having taken
a programming course, he found he has a knack for computers and spends time at school and at home programming. After a long session at the computer, he wants to be
alone. He sits absent-mindedly at the dinner table, unable
to join in the conversation. He feels exhausted. He looks
forward to going to his room to rest and recuperate. Sometimes he falls asleep and dreams he's lost in a mass of
codes, cut off from other people. Then he wakes up,
startled.

David and Kenneth both suffer from a new kind of
disease: *technostress*. Technostress is a modern disease of
adaptation caused by an inability to cope with the new
computer technologies in a healthy manner. It manifests
itself in two distinct but related ways: in the struggle to
accept computer technology, and in the more specialized
form of overidentification with computer technology.

The primary symptom of those who are ambiva-
lent, reluctant, or fearful of computers is anxiety. This
anxiety is expressed in many ways: irritability, headaches,
nightmares, resistance to learning about the computer, or
outright rejection of the technology. Technoanxiety
most commonly afflicts those who feel pressured—by
employer, peers, or the general culture—to accept and
use computers.

Janice, for example, is a nurse in an intensive-care
unit. Recently, her hospital bought a computer system,
and now many of her record-keeping tasks have been computerized. For her, learning how to use the system was a

difficult and slow process, and she remains uncomfortable using it. Lately, she has had mixed feelings about the new technology; she knows that using the terminal more often will make it more familiar, but a part of her wants to avoid it altogether. She is plagued by nightmares in which she watches herself being swallowed up by a machine.

Tom is another victim of technology. An executive whose correspondence, reports, and other paperwork are increasingly computer-generated, he complains that it all seems so impersonal. Although he realizes it's a rather extreme—and expensive—measure, he insists that his secretary retype all his computer mail before he reads it.

There are many people, of course, who have greeted the spread of computers with enthusiasm. Some have managed to integrate the machines into their lives successfully. But high performance with high technology can exercise a dangerous influence on the human personality by encouraging a symbiotic relationship with the machine. The primary symptom among those who have too successfully identified with the computer technology—those for whom the computer has become the central core of existence—is a loss of the capacity to feel and to relate to others. Those in this technocentered state tend to be computer programmers and other professionals, but anyone who is intensely and constantly working or playing with computers is at risk. Technocentered people tend to be highly motivated and eager to adapt to the new technology. Unwittingly, however, they begin to adopt a mindset that mirrors the computer itself. Signs of the technocentered state include a high degree of factual thinking, poor access to feelings, an insistence on efficiency and speed, a lack of empathy for others, and a low tolerance for the ambiguities of human behavior and communication. At its most serious, this form of technostress can cause aberrant and antisocial behavior and the inability to think intuitively and creatively. In some cases spouses report that their technostress partners began to view them as machines. The wife of a director of computer services for a large

17

bank, for example, recalls that when they first met he was a warm, sensitive man. Today, he has no close friends, and his only recreational activity is watching television. He has no patience for the easy exchange of informal conversation. One night, she asked him to slow down as they walked home from a bus stop.

"Walk faster," he replied.

"I *can't* walk faster. My legs are shorter than yours."

"That's no excuse. You have to learn to walk more *efficiently,*" the husband replied.

For women, too, technostress can affect marital dynamics. Carol is a computer programmer who loves her work. She has been married for nine years. At home, her main topic of conversation is computers. "Especially after working on the computer, it takes her a few hours to come down to being a normal person," Jeremy, her husband, says. "Nothing I can do can bring her back to reality. She'll talk to me of routines and subroutines, and she never grasps the fact that I don't understand what she's talking about. So I sit and listen for a while, pretending I'm interested."

At first glance, many technocentered individuals do not seem troubled. They appear to have adapted successfully to their jobs, and whatever marital or other personal problems they are experiencing appear to be unrelated. In fact, they have sacrificed their psychological well-being for the predictable, rational, logical safety of a computerized environment. They are emotionally debilitated and often on the verge of exhaustion.


Like a stone plunging into a pond, the computer revolution has sent out shock waves of change. Its rings of influence have moved steadily outward, affecting more and more people. The technocentered person, numbed and cut off from humanity by constant contact with computers, is at the center. The computer-anxious person, baffled by

18

conflicts and worried about the effects of the computer at work and at home, is also grappling with frequent computer contact. But all of us suffer its repercussions. Even if we have never touched a keyboard, we cannot escape technostress. Ordinary social relations, daily chores, and dreams for the future are affected by machinery on which we are increasingly dependent, and of which we are increasingly wary. Consider the following vignettes:

Anne is waiting to buy a plane ticket at the airport. An automated ticket machine has been installed in the past year. Customers insert their credit cards, punch in their flight information, and wait a few seconds for the ticket to be printed out; a ticket agent is unnecessary. The person in front of Anne is unfamiliar with the procedure and is taking a few extra seconds to read the instructions. "How can people be so stupid," Anne thinks to herself. She feels impatient and irritated, even though she knows there is plenty of time until her flight.

Bill is a researcher who frequently works until closing time at the library. Often he is late coming up to the desk to check out his book. Usually, he can persuade the librarian to help him out. Recently, the library bought a computerized checkout system. The first time Bill tried to check books out after the official closing time the librarian told him there was nothing she could do—the system simply wouldn't accept the procedure. "I started to yell at the librarian," Bill recalls, "which is unusual for me." Because the computer had erased the normal social bond between librarian and patron, Bill felt no compunctions about taking his anger out on the librarian.

It is not necessary to have a computer-based job in order to suffer from one form or another of technostress. Most of us are either a little technoanxious or a little technocentered. In the midst of celebrating the new bond between people and machines, we feel a vague sense of helplessness about the steady inroads computers are making in our lives: the whoops and boings of video games in restaurants and movie theaters; voice-synthesis chips imbedded in car dashboards that remind us to close the door; and, on a more sinister level, automated missile alert systems, which already have had a few well-publicized malfunctions.

Our glorification of logic machines and the experts who give them orders is changing our standards of normalcy: behavior once regarded as cold and undesirable we may now view as industrious, admirable, intriguing, even heroic. The computer nerd has been transformed into the computer wizard, profiled in business magazines, sought after by the Pentagon, dramatized in films.

Hollywood, always ready to exploit a popular anxiety, has cast renegade computers as the featured villains in such movies as *Superman III, War Games,* and *Tron.* (In a case of life imitating fiction, in 1983 a cabal of adventure-seeking Milwaukee high school students, the "414s," inspired in part by the plot of *War Games,* penetrated sensitive computer networks at the Sloan-Kettering Cancer Institute and Los Alamos Scientific Laboratory, even going so far as to program one computer to greet users with a line from the movie—"Would you like to play a nice game of chess, Dr. Falken?")

No more visible symbol of the computer in our daily lives exists than the rapidly proliferating twenty-four-hour push-button banking machines, and they are not always greeted by customers with delight. When Citibank in New York announced it was restricting access to human tellers and substituting banking machines conveniently located in lobbies outside, the outcry revealed the public's uneasiness with the trend. And inevitably, some people did more than protest: a disgruntled customer in Florida fired six rounds from a .32-caliber pistol into a cash machine when it confiscated his bank card. "It was the second time it's happened to me, and I've only been down here four months," the man told the Associated Press. "I got a little upset."

*   *   *

To blame the computer itself for causing technostress would be simplistic; after all, it is not the mere existence of the machine that creates problems. Situational stress is, and always has been, a common ingredient of life. Stress is the tension we feel when we try to adapt—whether changing jobs, getting married, learning to drive, or moving to a new home, all the while struggling to regain our old equilibrium.

In order to understand technostress, we need to distinguish between two types of adaptation, simple and complex. Simple adaptation means adjustment to patterns that leave the composition of the self unchanged, and implies only the adoption of a new habit. An example is the change from a traditional diet of meat, eggs, and cheese to one of vegetables, cereals, and fruits. People worried about high cholesterol will adapt to this new pattern, but this adaptation will have little if any effect on their personalities; it does not normally alter their outlook on life or their social relationships. Simple adaptations are frequent.

Complex adaptation occurs under more drastic circumstances—for example, when children leave home to attend school for the first time. They must be able to muster enough independence to meet a new authority and to come to terms with new demands on them. When they adapt to the necessities of the new situation, something happens inside them; the way they think and feel about the world changes. They experience their lives in new ways after mastering the new situation. Their sense of self is altered.

Complex adaptation is stressful. Stress in itself is not necessarily bad; it is a natural response of the organism to challenge and a little stress is normal, even healthy. Recent medical studies suggest that some types of stress may cause the body to release chemicals that promote a sense of well-being and prevent diseases. This may help to explain why fast-moving executives seem to thrive in stressful situations. Beyond a certain threshold, however, the struggle to make complex adaptations becomes too costly, and stress becomes harmful. It can provoke anxiety, depression, irritability, low self-esteem, and other problems. Often the damage shows up in psychosomatic ailments: headaches, muscle tension, shortness of breath, peptic ulcers.

Such situational illnesses are the hallmark of the twentieth century. Our very ways of life can be fatal. High-cholesterol diets have been linked to heart disease; cigarette smoking to lung cancer. Even personality itself can be life-threatening. Two San Francisco cardiologists, Meyer Friedman and Ray Rosenman, have observed that certain personality traits—impatience, competitiveness, high job involvement, a sense of urgency, and other characteristics of what they dubbed the "Type A personality" —seem to correlate with heart disease. Recent studies indicate that this personality type can be acquired: working in a fast-paced, high-pressure job, an easygoing, low-key Type B personality who begins to feel inadequate or unable to maintain control can suffer from the same health problems as a Type A person.

Adaptation to computers is complex. A very fine line separates successful adaptation and technostress. Whether technostress results from an individual's effort to adapt to computers is ultimately determined by an interplay of personal and situational factors.

Unfortunately, the wholesale, rapid computerization of our society has created an enormous and sudden need to adapt to new lifestyles, relationships, and routines. The everyday problems that people normally experience— marital disputes, loneliness, job dissatisfaction, boredom —are aggravated in a world where computers increasingly substitute for humans. The resulting tension not only changes personality and behavior, but pushes us beyond the threshold of manageable stress. We are basically creatures of change. As children we experience a tremendous rate of change and are not really stressed by it; in fact, it enhances our psychological growth. As adults we seek novelty in our work and in our personal lives. Technostress is not simply an expression of our resistance to change. It is a reaction to the content of that change.

Our inexperienced and often improper preparation for living with computers is a central source of techno-stress, whether it's the novice computer user's uneasiness with machine logic or the technocentered expert's annoyance with human inefficiency. There are no generations of retired computer users whose advice we can seek and examples we can follow. We are our own guinea pigs.

The French sociologist Jacques Ellul recognized thirty years ago that the coming technological age was an irresistible force "imposed by economic considerations." In the face of this force, he predicted, man would either remain as he was—unadapted, neurotic, and inefficient— or adapt with "a tremendous effort of psychic mutation." The first signs of a massive cultural mutation are becoming evident. In a society already plagued by stress-related illnesses, from hypertension to cancer, technostress may be the most crucial disease we have ever had to face.

# TWO

## The Mental Sweatshop

"If I get more productive I'm going to scream."

*Janice*
Legal secretary

THE SHOCK TROOPS of the computer revolution are the secretaries, accounts receivable clerks, bookkeepers, directory assistance operators, travel agents, and order clerks for whom technostress is becoming a fact of life. Indeed, a 1981 study by the National Institute of Occupational Safety and Health (NIOSH) showed that clerical workers who use computers suffer higher levels of stress than any other occupational group—including air traffic controllers.

The main battlefield in the struggle to adapt to technology is the newly automated office. The next decade will see further expansion of the information economy, and the computer will contribute even more to this growth than the railroad did to the infrastructure of the industrial economy. The computer and the work it generates have created not merely a new era in history but with it a new psychological space as well.

The term "personal space" became popular in the 1960s to denote the psychological turf that people felt they needed to control if they were to be content. The phrase usually came up when partners in a relationship sought to regulate distance and closeness. By the 1970s, the concept of personal space became a part of an ongoing relationship between two people.

In the 1980s the key to controlling one's life has more to do with electronic space than personal space. Electronic space is the psychological field that people find themselves inhabiting when their thoughts and activities are shaped by their involvement with computer technology. This psychological field need not be determined by the technology directly. Rather, like gravity, the computer sets up a force field, the effects of which can be felt but not seen. For example, the computer generates new procedures and new divisions of labor that affect people who never actually sit down at a computer terminal. The closer one is to the computer, the more dense the field.

Electronic space is divided into two zones. The private zone, where we depend on computers to perform tasks affecting our private life—banking, telephones, billing systems—and the production zone, where we depend on computers to perform our work. Both zones affect us, but since computers are more likely to be a constant presence in the production zone, it is here that we find ourselves influenced by computers most drastically.

In electronic space, the dominant activity is information processing. Those doing the processing are generally referred to euphemistically as "knowledge workers." The title conjures up wisdom, respect, and authority, but this only obscures the fact that electronic-office workers toil under as much pressure and with as little control over their work as any sweatshop laborer. To be sure, there are rewarding jobs to be had in the electronic workplace— lawyers, executives, teachers, accountants. And, given the retrenching in such traditional sectors of the economy as manufacturing and agriculture, more and more of the nation's labor force is joining the high-tech information-processing sector. The reality of the computerized workplace, nevertheless, is that the vast majority of employees are expected to carry out routine, repetitive, uninteresting, and alienating chores day after day.

The electronic workplace is a relatively new phenomenon, and as a result human casualties until recently have been too few to be noticed. The first large-scale computer applications, for military and scientific work, took place barely forty years ago. In the postwar years, government agencies and private corporations bought and installed their own computers. New and expensive, they were purchased in the hope of reducing costs. The state of the art was then vacuum-tube technology with magnetic tape-drives, rudimentary operating systems, and tedious machine-language programming—stone age technology, from today's vantage point.

In the business world of the 1950s, these cumbersome devices were used for repetitive, well-defined accounting chores. Computer operations were tightly centralized, with programming carried out by small cadres of computer experts. Their major impact was on a distinct group of clerical workers whose main tasks included inputting and sorting data. In their daily tasks, the majority of employees throughout the company remained largely unaffected by the technology.

The second expansion came in the 1960s. Huge volumes of data were processed, but the computers were still used primarily in a routine fashion for such tasks as inventory control, payroll, and billing. By the end of the decade computer use had spread into new realms of business: airline reservations, credit-card processing, securities tracking. By this time transistors had replaced vacuum tubes, and tapes and discs had replaced punch cards. Programming languages were simpler. Still, the computer operators within an organization remained a small and specialized group.

In the 1970s companies began to allocate funds for information processing and to use computers for new and vital functions: decision-making, financial planning, and management. Information itself began to be viewed as an important part of a company's resources, like its personnel or raw materials. This was the heyday of the data processing department, whose members held the key to crucial facts and figures. But despite the increasing dependence of the company on data, managers and general staff viewed the computer from a distance.

Today, in the era of the microchip, high tech reigns. Computers are cheap and often tiny. One microcomputer can handle the functions of a complicated and expensive array of office equipment. The realm of jobs that are now done by computers has expanded; the duties and judgments of white-collar workers (and, increasingly, managers) have been programmed into it. Many workers, scattered throughout the company, spend hour after hour typing on computer keyboards, monitoring printouts or reading VDTs. Many, if not most, of these people had never touched a computer five years ago.

With this expansion, clerical and white-collar employees must now perform what were once familiar tasks, such as typing, writing, and filing, at an accelerated pace. They must process more information and learn new languages and routines in order to accomplish their customary jobs. In the past, companies were unable to accurately monitor or standardize workers' output; now they can calculate such minute statistics as how many pieces of paper a typist might use to type a letter, or how long it took an employee to read two reports and six memos.

The industrial model of production that has traditionally been used on the assembly line has moved into the office. The efficiency expert has been replaced by the productivity engineer, but their goal is identical. Early efficiency studies were time and motion studies, and the limits to production were largely the limits of strength and speed in the human body. Today's efficiency studies are essentially time and thought studies, and the limits to production are those of the human brain and nervous system. Even mental processes—for example, the learning of new procedures—are now measured and standardized. Despite increasing evidence that human beings cannot perform according to mathematical equations and formulas, the productivity engineer tends not to take into consideration such individual and sometimes intangible human elements as perception, motivation, and emotional state. Instead, a mechanistic model of the worker is matched with the computer; it is assumed that the combination will mean an automatic and trouble-free increase in productivity. A nightmarish vision of human workers as "materials" is conjured in the following statement by Robert Boguslaw, a leading computer systems engineer:

> We must take care to prevent . . . [a] . . . single-sided analysis of the complex characteristics of one type of systems materials, namely human beings. What we need is an inventory of the manner in which human beings can be controlled and a description of some of the instruments that will help us achieve that control. If this provides us with sufficient handles on human materials so that we can think of them as metal parts, electrical power, or chemical reactions, then we have succeeded in placing human materials on the same footing as any other materials and can begin to proceed with our problems of system design.

30

As the rhythm of the workplace speeds up to match that of the computer, the resulting increase in both load and rate of work, aggravated by the reliance on symbols and abstractions that the computer demands, creates new physical and psychological pressures. Our reaction to these pressures is expressed in the symptoms of technostress. Extending ourselves beyond our natural limits has taken a considerable toll:

Alice, a claims processor for an insurance company, works at a computer all day. By midday she has trouble focusing her eyes and suffers muscle aches and pains in her shoulders, forehead, and neck. She is tense and irritable at the close of the day, and when she returns home her only desire is to be left alone to recuperate. Yet Alice is productive; the stress she feels has not yet hampered her performance.

Maxine is in her early fifties. She sits all day at a computer processing inventories, struggling to concentrate while trucks thunder past on the freeway outside the office. Although she isn't conscious of it, the terminal is also emitting a high-pitched hum. At home, even the smallest sounds set her off. If she hears music in a neighbor's apartment, or even a toilet flushing in the building, she complains to the superintendent. Her extreme sensitivity to noise stems from her work environment.

Alice and Maxine are not isolated cases. A poll of 1,263 office workers in 1982, sponsored by Verbatim Corporation, a manufacturer of floppy discs, revealed that 63% were concerned about eyestrain and 36% were concerned about backstrain. Nearly eight in ten respondents called for better lighting and 79% called for periodic rest breaks. Many of the workers polled noted that management seldom consulted them on the design of their work spaces or the structuring of their workday. Recently, an International Federation of Information Processing Workers panel suggested that the mental hazards "caused by inhumanely designed computer systems should be considered a punishable offense," as are physically hazardous working conditions.

Recently, in the *New England Journal of Medicine,* a group of professionals warned that prolonged gazing at colored phosphorous screens can induce a psychological phenomenon known as the "McCollough effect." After looking at green letters on a VDT screen for several minutes, people begin to see pink-colored letters when they then look at type on a black-and-white screen. If an amber screen is used, the tint of the letters on a black-and-white screen will appear blue-green.

Although the researchers call the McCollough effect a "harmless physiological curiosity," they felt compelled to advise physicians "not to mistake it for a hysterical symptom or a manifestation of neurological disease." Although it may be harmless, it is nevertheless disturbing to users who often believe it to be caused by their inability to adapt to computers, or are suspicious of the physical consequences of working with VDTs.

In 1981, NIOSH compiled a study based on questionnaires submitted to 250 VDT operators and 150 nonoperator control subjects at five work sites. Although little difference in psychological mood was reported between the groups, clerical VDT operators reported higher levels of job stress and health complaints than did professional VDT operators and control subjects. The clerical workers complained of visual, musculoskeletal, and emotional problems. The study concluded: "a number of interacting factors (job content, task requirements, workload) and environmental factors (lighting, work station design) contributed to the observed levels of job stress and health complaints." It added that the work system "imposed" by VDTs possibly added to the health problems.

32       Several studies in Europe have corroborated the NIOSH findings. They indicate that the usual keyboard layout causes constrained posture that could lead to physical ailments. Pains in the neck, shoulders, and arms have been consistently reported in studies of keypunchers, typists, and even cashiers. In an enormous sample of 16.9 million workers in Japan, assembly line workers and certain office employees frequently complained of shoulder and arm pain. The Japanese authors of the study coined the term "occupation cervicobrachial syndrome" to describe the ailment. For some workers the pain continues even when they switch jobs and are no longer using those particular muscles.

The physical symptoms of fatigue among computer workers are also numerous—weariness, headaches, burning eyes, neck pains—and so too are the causes of that fatigue. Sources of discomfort include such factors as uncorrected eyesight problems, bad posture, general ill health, or alcoholism. Age is also a consideration; visual performance, for example, drops noticeably between the ages of thirty and fifty. But many sources of fatigue relate to the computer itself: the keyboard arrangement, VDT character size and readability, picture quality and brightness. Other factors have to do with the general work environment: duration of uninterrupted work periods, degree of concentration required, freedom to pause at will, use of documents and other job aids, office illumination, and so on.

Study after study has debated the pros and cons of

sitting at a computer console, hour after hour, day after day. Much of the controversy has focused on the possibility of actual physical damage. Since the 1970s, workers have been concerned that radiation from the terminals may cause cataracts and birth defects. These concerns have lingered even though NIOSH and other researchers have repeatedly said there is no radiation hazard. This has become the subject of heated discussion between manufacturers and unions, with manufacturers charging that the unions were harping on the issue only as an organizing tactic. Unions, on the other hand, have criticized manufacturers for not taking the problem seriously enough.

More than a dozen bills were introduced in 1983 in at least six states to regulate the manufacture or use of keyboards and screens. So far, none of the proposed legislation has passed. But many observers expect a change as public interest rises. Already, the Swedish and West German governments have issued standards for VDT design and use. To prevent similar intervention in the U.S., the Computer and Business Equipment Manufacturers Association formed a task force in early 1983. Its aim is to present state legislatures with findings that, according to Vico E. Henriques, the association's president, leave allegations of health hazards "unproved or disproved."

A NIOSH-sponsored study of VDT complaints carried out recently by the National Research Council concluded that it was a matter of "annoyance to workers" rather than a public health problem. NIOSH promptly rejected that conclusion and vowed to continue investigating the issue. Dr. Lawrence Stark, a neuro-opthalmologist at the University of California at Berkeley, was a member of the National Research Council's VDT panel. After the report was released, Stark was quoted as saying, "It was a good summary, but I disagreed with the general philosophy of the report. Just because visual fatigue is not scientifically well defined does not negate the fact that there is fatigue. And even though it is difficult to define the requirements for a good VDT, no VDT is as good as a piece of paper." In one month in 1983, a toll-free "VDT Risks Hotline" set up by 9to5, a working women's organization located in Boston, recorded about a hundred phone calls daily from office personnel, whose complaints ranged from burning eyes to difficulty in focusing.

Although we cannot be sure of the long-term physical dangers, we know that many physical discomforts result from working closely with VDTs. And, perhaps more important, mental fatigue, which is every bit as debilitating as physical fatigue, has been strongly in evidence in the kinds of job stress suffered by computer workers.

34

Jane is a clerical worker in a large insurance company that computerized its operations several years ago. The new setup includes an electronic mail system, and Jane essentially works in a paper-free environment. She is distressed by the unexpected ways the equipment has altered her work cycle. Her production rates are monitored, she is frequently behind schedule, and her day is filled with perfunctory tasks that, because of the sensitivity of the computers and the speed of information flow, require a high degree of concentration. She feels tense and under pressure all the time, and no longer looks forward to her workday.

White-collar workers these days are experiencing a great deal of culture shock. Traditionally, office workers prided themselves on being a cut above the blue-collar labor force. The office clerical job, although routine, was once something of a prestige position, in contrast to mill or factory work. Even those in the predominantly female "pink-collar ghetto"—secretaries, receptionists, typists—considered themselves skilled workers. Computers are weakening this perception. With the advent of the electronic office, these employees often worry that their jobs are being reduced to those of machine attendants, with less room for initiative, variety, and creativity than ever before. For many people this signifies a demotion. However stressful the computer job may be, the sense of backsliding makes it worse.

Karen Nussbaum, one of the directors of the National Association of Working Women, described in *Technology Review* a job she once had at an insurance company. "I typed one green form all day long," she recalls. She worked in a huge room with about two hundred other workers. "I had thousands of green forms. I typed the same series of symbols—codes, usually not even whole words—into the computer. I typed that in boxes at the top and then further on down. Nobody even told me what the point was."

The entry of computers into an office can indeed mark a psychological turning point for many workers. Not only are well-practiced skills suddenly obsolete, but traditional sources of dissatisfaction are aggravated by the introduction of technology. The current generation of workers are better educated, better informed, and have higher expectations than did previous generations. They seek jobs that give not only a sense of accomplishment but a sense of purpose, jobs that provide meaningful work. The new host of technological assembly-line jobs frequently provide anything but that. As a way of compensating, companies give the simplest of jobs impressive technical titles, but cosmetic improvements don't remove the underlying stress of working at a job that retains its routine elements.

Kevin is a "systems sundry specialist" in a San Francisco office. The title doesn't change the fact that he's an order clerk. Nor does it change the intrinsic boredom of his job. "I wanted for the longest time to get away from all the paper," Kevin says. "We were really bogged down in it. Now that we've done away with the paper I'm being driven nuts with symbols on the screen. I can't win for losing."

It is not just the office, of course, that is host to this new knowledge proletariat. The computer industry's rapid growth is due in part to the demand for computers by hospitals, airlines, retailers, restaurants, travel agencies, libraries, and other service businesses. Many of the stresses found in the automated office have thus spread into the service sector. Waiters, sales clerks, and other service workers are often initially drawn to their jobs because they consider themselves "people people." They take pride in their interpersonal skills and satisfaction in giving customers personal attention—the heart of any service job. As in the office, the computer is changing all this. Employees find themselves "interfacing" with computers, rather than interacting with people. The low-level computer jobs all begin to seem the same, from one end of the economy to the other: computer operator. The resulting technostress among service workers is much the same as it is for their counterparts in the office.

Nancy works as a waitress. A computerized cash register has recently been installed in the restaurant where she works. Although she has been shown a number of times how to operate the register, she is unnerved by its speed and sensitivity. She has become impatient with her usual customers, is slow to give change, and generally feels dissatisfied with her job. She is currently looking for another waitressing job at a restaurant with an old-fashioned cash register.

Many of us had a difficult enough time at school learning new math, memorizing the dates of history lessons, and writing essays using correct grammar. Now, in a short time, with our livelihoods at stake, we must prepare to operate complex machines, solve problems in new ways, memorize a raft of new procedures, and perhaps even learn programming languages. We are accustomed to learning by trial-and-error, but using this method to absorb the new technology can be costly and sometimes disastrous, as anyone knows who has ever lost a whole day's work by the simple push of a wrong button.

The stress of anticipating the change that technology will bring, as well as the experience of learning about it when it arrives, can burden even a highly motivated employee. It can linger long after he or she has learned to use or even like the computer.

Mary, who has been an executive secretary for ten years, was recently was told that a professional work station would be installed in her office. She has begun to worry about the future of her position with the company and the ways in which her relationship with her employer will change. She is irritable with her co-workers, less interested in her work, and thinks about quitting. She is preoccupied at home with events at work, finds it difficult to relax with her husband, and has begun suffering from recurring headaches.

Novice computer users sometimes end up feeling that since the technology is perfect, they are to blame for their failure to grasp new procedures immediately. They begin to experience painful self-doubts. Some employees handle this by going on an emotional sit-down strike. They quietly refuse to learn anything significant about the technology, and skip over assigned chores.

Michelle works for a law firm as a paralegal secretary. She prides herself on her fast and accurate work, and sees the firm's recently installed word-processing system as a threat to her arduously acquired skills. Her terminal sits at her desk, unused and ignored, as she continues to use her electric typewriter. She has used the word processor only when her employer insists.

The replacement of a typewriter with a letter-quality computer printer can be a traumatic experience. After years on a job, office workers begin to regard their workspaces as their own; like a carpenter's hammer, the typewriter becomes a part of their lives and an extension of their bodies. Computerization can feel like an invasion of personal turf; sometimes the emotional reaction to this trauma can be quite severe, and rejection turns into sabotage.

Bonnie, for instance, was a secretary at an educational research center in California's Silicon Valley. When computers were installed in the office and training sessions held for the staff, she was conspicuous in her refusal to learn how to use them. When her terminal later broke down, a repair technician found that coffee had apparently been poured into it. Bonnie was subsequently fired.

One executive at Blue Shield of Massachusetts boasted to the *Wall Street Journal* that in some cases, productivity had tripled once departments were computerized. But a claims processor told the same reporter that the workers considered the office a sweatshop; none of them expected to remain for more than two years.

Employees are quick to notice how drastically the computer changes their jobs. The stress this causes is further aggravated when management pressures workers to learn the new systems, without letup in productivity, and then increases their workloads as soon as they are acquainted with the system. Most managers have no idea how to manage the introduction of computer technology. They are so caught up in the promise of productivity that they forget how much has to change if people are to work comfortably and effectively. In addition, managers must contend with their own technological anxieties. Ironically, they seem to be implementing computers in such a way as to virtually guarantee technostress:

1. They think computers can solve problems that are at their core personnel issues: labor tension, poor morale, or falling productivity.
2. They assume that all employees are capable of learning the technology at the same rate.
3. They keep workloads high while people attempt to master new tasks and procedures.
4. They introduce the computers with little or no notice or preparation.
5. They hover over employees during the introductory period, all too frequently pointing out only their mistakes.
6. They keep policies regarding retraining or layoffs secret, thus fueling rumors.

7. They scold employees for using older, informal networks for information gathering.
8. They delegate the entire responsibility for implementing the new computer system to lower-level managers.
9. They don't invite employees to participate in deciding how the new system will be used. Instead, they stick closely to corporate directives.
10. They reduce funds for training personnel to an absolute minimum.

These rules reflect the old industrial model in action—an attitude that makes it difficult for people in the organization to adapt appropriately to computers. It betrays a disregard for the psychological integrity of the individual, to say nothing of the complexity of the change itself.

Management needs to address the realities of the technological invasion of the workplace. Unless we are given the opportunity to express and resolve this issue, we remain vulnerable to varying levels of technostress. Increased sensitivity on the manufacturer's part is also called for; in their efforts to downplay the complexities of their products, computer companies have cut after-sale support services that previously aided office workers in learning about the new equipment.

The implementation of technology is of itself sufficient cause for worker stress. Yet for many employees the serious trouble is still to develop. Once the introductions are over, the experience of adaptation—for employer and employee—begins in earnest. That experience tends to involve five processes: increased mental workloads, distortion of time, loss of control, social isolation, and disappointment.


The electronic workplace appears calm. There is not much movement within the softly lit work stations, and there is little of the customary clatter of industry. But a significant change has taken place: mental workloads and mental fatigue are greater than they have ever been before. Personnel giving stock quotes to shareholders in one brokerage house, calling up information from desktop units, are expected to handle one call every ninety seconds. A minimum of 80,000 keystrokes per hour is expected of the average VDT operator, as compared to 30,000 keystrokes expected of the average secretary. An architect using computer-aided design (CAD) makes nineteen times more decisions per hour than does a pencil-wielding colleague, according to design engineer Michael Cooley. Within the apparent serenity of these sleek work stations, the burden of work is more wearying than at any point in history.

Philip was part of a team at a large bank that developed a computer program to pay savers their interest automatically on the first day of each month. The task was completed to everyone's apparent satisfaction, and most members of the team were reassigned to new projects. Due to a fluke the day before the first automatic payments were to be disbursed—a favored customer was handed his computerized check a day early—it was discovered that the bank was about to overpay everyone as much as double the interest due them. At 6:00 P.M., Philip, the only remaining analyst assigned to the project, was called in. The project manager came. His manager came. The vice president came. An estimated eight to ten million dollars in bank funds were on the line, to be disbursed when the doors opened for business the next morning. Philip had to find the flaws in his team's program and develop an algorithm to withdraw the appropriate amount from each account.

Unfortunately, such stories are not unusual in the computerized business world. Computers bring centralization, and centralization magnifies mistakes. One inappropriate line of code can cause a blackout, abort a NASA mission, misdirect a fortune, or mail millions of brochures to the wrong people. And with computerization, events occur so quickly that there is often no time at all to remedy a mistake. Even when mistakes are not made, the knowledge that all parts of a company are now tightly interdependent weighs heavily on the minds of the workers at each department. Stomach troubles and headaches become epidemic; workers are unable to relax even during slack periods of a production cycle.

Questions of organization aside, when management introduces computers, workers invariably feel new pressure to produce. The quantification of tasks that the computer engenders leads to added monitoring of each worker. To a degree, this pressure is often internalized. Technical workers, especially those who take pride in their work, push themselves harder than ever to match the efficiency and tirelessness of the computer. The result is often not greater productivity but bleary eyes, headaches, and rising error rates. Interacting with a computer is always an exhausting activity, even over a short period, and mental fatigue becomes a familiar feeling for the technostressed individual.

As technostress sets in, workers try to keep functioning as effectively as possible by concentrating only on the task at hand. Intolerance for interruption is one of the basic symptoms of technostress, felt by programmer and fill-in keyboard person alike. The computer demands concentration, and the worker responds with total absorption: the fingers, keys, and cursor seem to merge. Part of the abhorrence of interruption stems from the importance of short-term memory to the computer user. To operate a computer, we must commit an array of specific commands and procedures to memory—the sequence of twelve keys needed to call up a file from the previous day, or the eight keys needed to move a block of text. Unlike long-term memory, which helps us recognize a celebrity's face, or spell "Europe" correctly, short-term memory is quickly filled up. Most of us can recall only a handful of recently learned numbers, letters, words, or procedures. Interruptions threaten to jar loose the imperfectly stored data we must recall in order to operate a computer program. Because in a typical job new computer systems and procedures are constantly being updated, the facts we store in short-term memory rarely have a chance to graduate into long-term memory. The concentration thus needed to work with a computer is at odds with the easy sociability of many traditional workplaces.

Higher mental workloads force workers to pay close attention to immediate jobs and overlook creative alternatives. Computer workers faced with menial jobs have little chance to develop the cognitive skills of a craftsman. They can, at best, use their narrowly defined work skills to manipulate symbols and signs, their short-term memory to improve performance, and their error rate to judge themselves by. Technical workers with more complex duties than the entry-level operators are similarly limited in the kinds of skills they are called on to use and in the kinds of decisions they are allowed to make. They often complain about having too much data—they "don't know what to do with it all." More becomes the rule. Rather than thinking of genuinely different ways to carry out tasks or solve problems, they simply try to improve their speed and efficiency.

The concept of mental workload is an appropriate one in electronic space. Load, in physics, refers to something that imposes a burden on a structure. In computer work, the structure in question is the human brain, and too many companies tend to view the brain as just that, a structure that accommodates measurable loads. But scientists have data correlating increased workload with computerization. Pupillary dilation is an observable indicator of mental activity, and already studies exist that correlate pupillary dilation and computer-related work. No more important ingredient of technostress exists than mental overloading and fatigue. Exhaustion lowers the body's defenses to physical disease, as it lowers the brain's resistance to technostress.

Another ingredient of technostress, and one closely

42

related to mental workload, is the apparent acceleration of time. The worker internalizes the rapid, instant-access mode of computer operations, and the individual's inner sense of time distorts to accommodate the machine. Office workers become impatient with phone callers who take too long to get to the point. Travel agents drum their fingers in irritation as they wait to verify airline bookings—despite the near-simultaneity of request and reply, unheard of twenty years ago. Ultimately, and ironically, experienced users are stressed by the computer's own apparent slowness. A recent study showed that any response time longer than 1.5 seconds resulted in impatience on the part of users. (An exception is chess, where players matched against computers prefer a lag of at least three or four seconds so that they will have the impression of putting up a worthy fight.) Despite our daydreams of idyllic vacations where time is suspended, we have already internalized the fast pace of modern life. For the computer worker, the workday, with its routines and its repetitions, tends to drag just as much after computers are introduced as before. But within that monotony we are being deprived of our own ability to refuel, since the machine constantly and consistently demands our complete attention.

Karen, a typist, is required to produce a certain number of letters each day. Before her company introduced word processors she found her work demanding, but used the physical cue of removing the paper from her typewriter to remind her to take a break. Now, those cues are lost as she sits in front of a screen that has no natural end. She doesn't even take the time to chat with others in her office bay, since each typist is similarly absorbed in his or her duties. At the end of the morning she is exhausted, and wonders how she'll find the energy to complete the day's work.

Traditionally, while we work, there are moments when our minds are free and our thoughts wander from the task at hand. We imagine the future, rehearse responses, think about problems. Even workers engaged in seemingly mindless piece-work are allowed this luxury, evidenced by the comments of an assembly-line welder quoted by Studs Terkel in his book *Working:*

> You get involved with yourself. You dream, you think of things you've done. I drift back continuously to when I was a kid and what me and my brothers did. . . . Lots of times I worked from the time I started to the time of the break and I never realized I had even worked. When you dream, you reduce the chances of friction with the foreman or with the next guy. . . . If you were to think about the job itself you'd slowly go out of your mind. You'd let your problems build up, you'd get to the point where you'd be at the fellow next to you.

We need the opportunity to switch from one setting to the next, to forget a concern and give it time to pop back into the conscious mind later with a new perspective. It is by such processes that we reflect on our lives and sort out solutions. Unfortunately, the computer operator has little or no time for reflection. With this escape denied, irritability, fatigue, and dullness of spirit are unavoidable.

Another prime source of stress in the computerized workplace is the sense that control over our jobs, and thus our lives, is distant, centralized, and unyielding. At some American Express Company offices, a computer monitors the time taken by employees to answer the telephone. If there are more than three rings the computer notifies the supervisor. VDT operators at Blue Cross/Blue Shield in San Francisco have their keystrokes tallied automatically. Each time they get up to go to the bathroom, their count stops and their keystroke-per-hour rate dips. The mere fact that this kind of surveillance is being conducted promotes uneasiness and strain. Computer monitoring makes the already-resented time clock, which after all measures only one's physical presence, seem benevolent in comparison.

Ideally, supervisors observing their employees' output bring to their jobs understanding and empathy. But a computer does not take into consideration extenuating circumstances. Where once a supervisor might know that an employee has just returned from a bout with the flu, and thus is having an off day, the computer cannot see beyond its standardized expectations of productivity. Workers at a Volvo automobile plant pleaded with management to replace the computerized quality control with a human supervisor with whom they could discuss their evaluations and ratings. Workers elsewhere voiced similar misgivings:

Sue is a repair/service assistant at a telephone office in Kansas, where management periodically compiles "production studies" of each worker based on computer tallies of how many phone calls are answered and how much information is gathered per call. "So if you get a call from a friendly person who wants to chat, you have to hurry the caller off because it would count against you. It makes my job very unpleasant."

Alice is a supermarket cashier. Last month, her store installed electronic cash registers. One of the less publicized features of these machines is a built-in counter that transmits to a central terminal a running count of how many items each cashier has rung up that day. Alice has become self-conscious now whenever a customer strikes up a conversation with her, and she suppresses the desire to talk casually with customers herself. The situation has made her tense and resentful, and she finds herself thinking constantly about going home early.

Flexibility, improvisation, and initiative are pushed to the background as managers seek to raise their workers' efficiency by breaking down clerical tasks to "subroutines" that can be standardized and monitored. IBM, coiner of the term "word processing," has touted "word-processing centers" as a way to bring "manufacturing and production lines into the office." Secretaries, categorized as either correspondence or administrative secretaries, will find their "work divided, specialization introduced, and their job status raised," IBM promises.

Most of the clerical workers affected by the introduction of technology are women, employed in the "pink-collar" ghetto. Locked into low-status, low-paying jobs, many women have welcomed the opportunity to learn word processing, thus adding a new skill that would improve their career potential. Instead, they find that salaries drop as jobs are divided into a series of easily automated "subroutines."

Outside the clerical realm this new kind of control is also available to managers. In the airplane construction industry, for example, there are now software packages called parts programs that detail each step in assembling a section of a plane. The program dictates exactly how many seconds it should take a worker to tighten a particular bolt. If a construction team is missing its quotas, the program encourages management to measure the subroutines and ferret out the laggards. Without the computer, this kind of redefinition and accountability would be too cumbersome for a manager to attempt.

As jobs are broken up into smaller parts, job mobility suffers. Everyone is given a specialty, and movement from one specialty to another becomes more difficult.

Randy, a computer operator who tracks orders for a national clothing manufacturer, describes this process. "To move from my job of tracking orders to one of tracking those who track orders," Randy explains, "I need two programming languages, knowledge of two computer systems, and a minimum knowledge of system design. And you know what? That will only take me off the screen." The next job up the ladder will still be a tightly defined, routine one with little change in pay. Randy feels hemmed in and powerless, and blames the computer.

Traditionally, a combination of abilities was essential in skilled work. The furniture maker was a jack-of-all-trades: a connoisseur of wood and cloth, a carpenter, a woodcarver, an upholsterer, a merchant, and perhaps a weaver or fabric designer. Skills from one craft could translate into skills in another: painter Auguste Renoir began his career hand-painting ceramic plates; the Wright brothers built bicycles before they built airplanes. In the traditional business world, an ambitious young worker could find employment in a variety of departments in order to learn operations from the bottom up. In today's corporations, the "Renaissance man" has gradually given way to the technical specialist. As electronic space increases in density, the number of job functions multiplies, with system design personnel, support teams, implementation teams. Expertise in several areas is often no longer expected or encouraged. Once an office is computerized, software can theoretically substitute for much of a company's brainpower; people need only concentrate on knowing how to use the software. Employees feel their options sealed off; a sense for the organization as a whole, its workings, its tempo, its ethics, its goals, seems impossible to grasp in the face of a fragmented operation that appears on a computer screen. Workers feel stuck in dead-end jobs devoid of meaning. The alienation this produces, combined with the daily struggle to cope with the computer work itself, provides essential ingredients of technostress.

47

Another aspect of the rigid defining of jobs that often comes about with office centralization is a formalized power hierarchy. The computer must be programmed with precise rules as to who is allowed access to which files and who can monitor whose work. Passwords are assigned and special access codes distributed among the higher echelons. In smaller companies especially, this change can be unsettling. For example, office etiquette often decrees that we leave our desks unlocked at the end of the day, and our doors open when we make phone calls. We trust others not to steal into our work area and pilfer or sabotage files. With computerized passwords, we are forced to keep our work private, like it or not. Where the idea of secrecy may never have occurred to us—new filing cabinets always come with locks, but how many of us ever turn the key?—now we are forced to guard against theft and sabotage.

Similarly, just as traditional office etiquette dictates that supervisors ask employees to furnish needed files, now computerization pushes this unspoken rule aside. Supervisors simply call up by computer whatever materials they choose to examine, unannounced and undiscussed. Etiquette may not further efficiency, strictly speaking, but it does serve to oil the complex mechanism of interpersonal relations. When computerized flows supersede older forms of cooperation, the mood of an office changes in ways we never anticipated. Where once the workers may have seen themselves as members of a team working together, now they feel like troops in an army. The result reinforces the tension and stress of the automated office.

Walter is a magazine editor in a newly computerized office. Since the terminals have been wired up and passwords assigned, he has access only to his own stories and files and to the most general office information. To read the stories other people are working on or even to see typeset versions of his own stories beyond a certain point, he must "go through channels." Where he had once thought of himself as the managing editor's equal, he now realizes that he is a subordinate. The managing editor, after all, has access to Walter's files, but not vice versa. Walter feels demoralized and unappreciated. He chafes at his sense of being overcontrolled, and recalls wistfully the informality of the old office.

A common anxiety among those who operate computerized equipment is that the machine will literally end up controlling them. Production workers who now operate sophisticated computer-controlled machinery complain, "I don't pull the lever anymore, the machine does. My job is becoming rote. The machine isn't an extension of me—I'm just an extension of the machine."

Accomplishing a task becomes more and more a matter of following the steps of a program somebody else wrote. If the program has not yet been "debugged" and errors or delays result, the worker no longer has either the ability or the inclination to figure out what went wrong. This has serious effects on the satisfaction and dedication one brings to or derives from the job.

Some of the feelings of surrendering control are deceptive. In some ways the computer makes the user's job easier, as its designer intended. But as the worker becomes more and more dependent on the machine, there is a tendency to blame the computer itself for all problems that surface; there is less motivation to try to tackle problems via one's own initiative. "It's in the computer," the worker shrugs, "I can't do anything about it." Management may encourage these feelings by tightening its own control from above once the computers are brought in. Nevertheless, to a significant degree, the worker is in fact forced to relinquish control because of the structuring of the electronic workplace.

49

The solitary nature of computer work is another major source of technostress. From the typical worker's point of view, the workplace is much more than a place in which to work. It is an environment in which to make friends and to socialize, to share jokes, opinions, and plans. This is a vital part of most people's work experience, much as many managers may wish otherwise. "Goofing off" can become a problem in any office, yet informal chatting at work helps us stay in touch with what others are doing, view our own work from a broader perspective, gather second opinions on particular work-related problems, and recuperate from prolonged periods of focused work. Time at work constitutes half of our waking hours. To expect us to spend this time in isolation is to invite discontent and decreased productivity.

In electronic space, unfortunately, we are cut off from our co-workers more than ever before. With our clearly defined and detailed work routines, the need for contact with other workers—in fact, our very tolerance of those interactions—diminishes. The key interaction is between one worker and the computer. Talk becomes an irrelevant distraction. Our level of involvement with this so-called tool is more demanding than it ever was with pencil, typewriter, or adding machine. Because the computer's procedures are standardized, we must respond reliably and uniformly to its demands. Communicating by phone or on paper is now seen as too imperfect, too messy or too easy to misinterpret. The keyboard is safer.

50     Stan, now a West Coast computer store manager, is a former office manager who learned firsthand the problems of adaptation that workers face. He says that within two years of the introduction of computers, what had been a cheerful group of workers became "a pack of zombies." As a manager, he appreciated the increased seriousness, but he personally yearned for the good old days.

The computer keyboard has also replaced human interaction in sales. In some hardware stores customers can now walk up to the linoleum display and type in the particular product about which they want more information; a computer then displays it. Trade advertisements for this system point out that it will free salespeople to do what they do best—talking to people. In fact, it may free them to talk, but it will lessen the need. The salesperson becomes, in effect, an observer and stock clerk. Traveling sales reps now use portable personal computers with modems, or phone links, to the home office; they spend less time talking with the customer and more time relaying order information. The job has become depersonalized. Sales reps who prided themselves on their charm and affability now find those qualities less valued or needed.

Not surprisingly, interpersonal skills such as graciousness and tact diminish when data transfer, not conversation, is the preferred form of communication.

Peter, who works in a computerized insurance company office, believes that people in his office are no longer as friendly as they were before the office computerized its operations. There are fewer face-to-face meetings, and the electronic memos are brusquer than the old written ones. He recalls that one co-worker recently told another, via the terminals, "Anyone who could make a mistake like that ought to be fired." It is unlikely that the message would have been quite so blunt had it been transmitted by less impersonal means.

In 1983, *Psychology Today* documented the increase in "flaming"—making rude or obscene outbursts—by computer. According to the article, a study of group decision-making at Carnegie-Mellon University showed that students were more abusive to each other when the group was linked by terminal than when students met in person. We are less concerned with one another's feelings when we can't see the face or hear the voice at the other end. In more than one office, among the first pieces of electronic mail received after computers are installed is the high-tech version of the obscene phone call.

Obviously, talking by computer is no substitute for conversation. The computer does not allow for ambiguity, irony, or spontaneity. Even computers that are programmed to ask questions or inject a note of humor fall flat next to the richness of intonation and rhythm of human speech. With the computer, form distorts content. Instead of worrying about what we sacrifice when we replace traditional interaction with computer communication, we congratulate ourselves on the power and efficiency of the new system.

Along with increased mental workloads, distortion of time, loss of control, and social isolation, computer workers (and all other computer users) must grapple with disappointment. The reality of the computer's capabilities is often unequal to the expectations it kindles. Most of us have heard so much about how the computer will make our job easier that we've come to believe that our days of drudgery are past. Much to our dismay, however, and claims of user-friendliness aside, mastering the quirks of any particular system generally takes a certain amount of time, effort, guesswork, and outside help.

By her second day on the job as a typist, Cindy found herself utterly stumped by the word-processing system. The user's manual provided no clue as to what she was doing wrong, and no one in the office that day could help her. She was expecting the word processor to make her job easy, but she tearfully explained to a co-worker that it takes two days to carry out what is supposed to be a five-hour job.

Hardware and software companies have begun to acknowledge the complexity of their products. "Help" buttons, error messages in plain English, better graphic displays, and more civilized users' manuals have all been improvements. One company has even offered an 800 "help" number for home computer users who get stuck. But the technology can still be too baffling and difficult for comfort.

Computers have traditionally been accompanied by manuals full of technical instructions that sometimes seem designed primarily to drive people crazy. Or, if they are relatively easy to read, it is at the expense of brevity. As a result, many novices skip over whole sections of manuals and attempt to learn the software on their own. For those who tend to take an intuitive approach to information, this is particularly frustrating. Impatient with the linear format of the manual, they feel defeated when they discover that their own rules cannot be applied in learning the system.

Disappointment can stem from other kinds of false expectations as well. Just as office workers welcomed the arrival of typewriter correction tape as an improvement over opaquing fluid, so office workers now look to word processors to free their manuscripts from all traces of correction. The "delete" button is indeed a marvel, until the first time an elbow hits it by accident and two hours' worth of typing is lost. And instant, perfect corrections don't necessarily free the worker for that fabled extra cup of coffee.

Sarah's boss has assured her that using the word processor will ease up and accelerate her writing chores. She has found instead that although in some respects her work does go faster, her boss constantly asks her to make small deletions and insertions on final documents. He tells her all she has to do is print out a new version, as if the computer were doing all the additional work by itself.

One has to wonder how much the electronic printer, like the Xerox machine that created new mounds of paperwork to read and store, actually advances the cause of office efficiency.

Ultimately, workers in the electronic office either sink or swim. If they fail—willfully or involuntarily—to adapt to the new technology, they wind up unemployed. If they learn to carry out their tasks in the new environment, most of the early anxieties and pressures dissipate and they achieve a functional equilibrium.

Successful adaptation generally takes about a year. There are a number of signs that workers have reached this stage. They begin to regard the computer as a perfectly natural part of their worklife and can't imagine doing their job without it. Workers using a word processor, for example, invariably can't imagine using correction fluid again. If they are forced to use a typewriter because the computer is "down," they find the typewriter aggravatingly slow. Its output lacks the pristine quality of the computer's; it has become obsolete. This attachment to the technology is the most telling sign that resistance is over.

The computer now determines the flow of work through the office, and the staffers set their work rhythms to fit the computer's pace. People expect a faster flow of reports, with fewer visible errors. Project times are compressed as less time is allowed for the automated parts of the job. A user-machine symbiosis develops. (One woman described her feelings toward her computer as maternal. Another worker, while preparing to move to a new location in the building, learned he could not take his beloved terminal with him. In a pique of anger he decided to take the terminal with him, and ripped its wires out of the wall.)

Adaptation does not come without a price. In some cases, establishing a working relationship with a computer is a Pyrrhic victory: the process of adaptation has changed the worker permanently. A study of workers at nine French electronics firms found that those who found their jobs most difficult were the ones who most strenuously resisted further job changes. Even when offered career advancement opportunities they were unwilling to accept a new position, because they had no desire to go through another "familiarization" phase with new equipment and new systems.

Workers who have adapted still remain vulnerable to the physical stress, increased mental load, eye strain, and uninterrupted work. And, with the constant onslaught of newer hardware and software, adaptation can never be truly complete. Technostress has become a way of life.

Not all sources of technostress relate directly to working with computers. There is a more abstract problem that troubles many technical workers and worsens the stress they are under: the fear of being automated out of a job. Since the days of *Modern Times*, Chaplin's film about assembly-line horrors, anxiety about automation's ultimate effect on jobs has been common. Speculation about unemployment in the long run is divided. Some say automation will free workers for new, more challenging, more creative tasks. Others foresee a new era of unemployment as American workers, underproductive and overpaid, are inevitably replaced by computers. While experts debate the question, the public at large is clearly uncertain about what to expect.

Newspapers are replete with stories about the development of new industries generated by the computer. The headlines read "Automated Offices Boom" and "Chip Manufacturers in Demand." The message is that new industries create new jobs, and the nation as a whole will benefit. That excitement is not supported by a glance at the rest of the news: a photo of an unemployed auto worker holding a sign that reads "Robots Don't Buy Cars"; a cartoon that depicts a personnel manager interviewing a robot: "No union demands, no sick time, no vacation pay? You're hired!"

55

Behind the uneasy laughter lurks panic. Workers and managers alike fear for their jobs when computers encroach on their tasks. Those activities that can be turned into algorithms and fed to computers are up for grabs. Thus, when the systems expert comes around to detail each person's job, employees claim that their tasks are too complex to capture in a flow chart. They hide information or try to dress up the complexity of the decisions they actually make, with the accent on the importance of experience and having a "feel" for how to do things right.

Employees who are not outwardly nervous may express their anxiety in other ways. They may have upsetting dreams: some see themselves all alone in a factory, with no companion except a machine. Others envision obsolescence, stranded in the middle of a large empty space. Still others dream about feeling ashamed once they are outmoded and can no longer provide for their families. Interestingly, fantasies of rising up and smashing the computers do not seem to be common, perhaps because we accept the computers' inevitability.

A manager describes the crux of the automation problem: "You employ two engineers and fifteen draftsmen in a precision metalworking foundry. Their job is to design the complicated parts from which molds will be taken. If you buy a computer with a plotter to do the designing, you will be able to employ a single person, an engineer, instead of seventeen."

On the most basic level, most workers suspect that they can be replaced by computers. It's just a matter of time, they say. An executive at General Motors quoted in Andre Gorz's book, *Farewell to the Working Class,* predicts that the traditional assembly line will have disappeared from American automobile factories by 1988. Factory equipment will be 90 percent computer-controlled, and only 50 percent of the unskilled work force will remain. As to the consequences of this re-equipment campaign, executives tend to be close-mouthed. It is easier for executives and workers to discuss plant closures and layoffs resulting from a sluggish economy than to admit that technology is making some workers' skills permanently useless.

Most economists are unfazed by the situation. Indeed, it is difficult to find a comprehensive investigation of the likely effects of massive automation on industrial employment. Most economists see the computer revolution as an extension of its industrial predecessor. Many workers, however, are unconvinced. They have noticed that companies implement the new machines even though the economy is not expanding. This, they reason, only throws people out of work. One young worker put it bluntly: "What do they expect us to do to eat properly? . . . You can't build a nation on data-crunching robots."

Thanks to the steady decline in the cost of computers, employers can now save on labor costs and capital investment at the same time. And the era of machines creating other machines is fast approaching. Robots will soon be producing other machines at knockdown prices. At Fujitsu Fanuc, a Japanese factory, one hundred workers produce an output that required five hundred workers in a traditional factory. In 1986 Fujitsu will employ two hundred people for an output that would have required twenty-eight hundred workers a few years ago. This trend will have a profound impact on American industry, which will be forced to keep pace.

Workers are not alone. Managers fear unemployment

as well. "American Management Ranks Overcrowded," warns a headline in the *Wall Street Journal*. Generally, however, they have an easier time handling unemployment than do the rank and file—at least in the short run. Managers are trained to think in terms of efficiency, and they can understand the business reasons for their dismissals. This perception helps cushion whatever personal defeat they may feel. Workers, on the other hand, tend to identify with their occupation or their union, rather than their company. The blow of losing a job is harder for them to rationalize. They tend to stay out of work longer and only some of them seek retraining.

57

For either category of employee, unemployment ultimately eats away at self-esteem. We normally spend much of our time discussing work, socializing with co-workers, and thinking about our jobs. We identify with the work we do. Status is earned according to what we do, how much we earn, and whether or not we supervise others, and, if so, how many. Our sense of worth, confidence, and security disappears when we lose our jobs.

Some observers take a benevolent view of unemployment. Harvard sociologist Daniel Bell, for example, says that in post-industrial society jobs lost in industry due to automation are not really a problem. Those displaced will follow the trends of the past and find jobs in the service sector. Bell's observation overlooks the profound hardships experienced by those unemployed workers forced to migrate from a factory job that paid ten dollars an hour plus benefits, to a service job at half the salary and few benefits. As one worker commented, "Working in a mill was no joyride, but working at McDonald's is like living the Depression—my wife and I both have to work just to make my old salary." As service jobs, too, are increasingly automated, these same workers feel squeezed once again, sensing their lack of skill in the new electronic economy. Many of them are uncomfortable working in customer relations or order departments. Working only with words and symbols is not the same as manual labor. "I can't get used to making a living filling out order blanks," comments one worker. "It feels like manipulation, not work."

Another benevolent view of automation asserts that the economy will open up vast numbers of technical jobs. Software programmers, designers, and engineers are all in demand. Opportunities for technical workers are likely to continue until the end of the century, comprising the solid center of the work force. However, as one worker points out, "We can't all be programmers."

58

Retraining is a complex issue psychologically as well as economically. People must be confident that they will be able to handle new jobs, such as programming, computer services, and engineering, that require upgrading skill levels. This confidence is, on the whole, lacking in an entire generation of workers displaced by computers and computer-controlled equipment. Barry Bluestone and Bennett Harrison, in *The Deindustrialization of America*, provide detailed evidence of the way in which advanced technology actually affects the labor force:

> Consider the 833,200 people in the New England . . . sample whose principal activity in 1958 was to work in the mill industries. In the period after 1958, as continuing deindustrialization swept through the sector, 674,000 of them left the mills. By 1975 only 18,000 of this group—fewer than 3 percent—were employed in the high-tech industry of the region (another 2,000 had migrated to high-tech jobs outside New England). More than five times as many ended up in trade and service jobs, either inside or outside the region. A huge number dropped out of the labor force (or went into jobs not covered by social security). In essence, losing one's job as a result of deindustrialization tends to propel one downward in the industry hierarchy toward lower productivity jobs—not upward.

In a computer-driven society, where a generation of

machines can be outmoded in twelve months and the knowledge needed for skilled jobs changes from one year to the next, aging is anathema. Middle age is seen as the last chance to secure a successful occupation or career. Tensions between the generations of job seekers are higher now than ever before in history. Competition for work is intense. Many job seekers find themselves either overqualified, as in the case of the laid-off welder who finds work as a cab driver, or underskilled, as are most blue-collar workers seeking to move into the developing computer trades. This makes for an era of profound identity crises.

Unemployment grows more stressful over time. Studies indicate that after four months out of work, people lose hope and depression sets in. And four months out of work is not an extreme situation: it has been estimated that nearly 40 percent of the unemployed remain so forty weeks or more. Boredom, frustration, and loneliness increase month by month. Almost two decades of psychological research have documented the stressful effects of unemployment: psychiatric problems, hypertension, cardiovascular illness, stomach problems, alcohol-related disorders, and high suicide and divorce rates. Clearly, subjective perceptions influence our health. (It is significant that when we feel control over our lives, we suffer less from disease. Unfortunately, the victims of automation rarely have a say in the outcome of the situation. They are seldom given the opportunity to experiment with alternatives, such as job sharing.)

The boom-and-bust cycles that wreaked havoc during the industrial era will exact more pain from individuals during the electronic era. Real after-tax income has been declining in recent years; working spouses and buying on credit are now the rule. We actually own only a small portion of the major purchases we make. We are more than ever dependent on our jobs. As a result, unemployment is more than a disturbing "down cycle"; it poses a real threat to our way of life and well-being.

Those who are absorbed by the high-tech industries will become highly specialized workers. This very specialization poses a new kind of risk for them. Their new skills are not readily transferable to other industries, or even to other narrow domains of the high-tech sector. Programmers who design games or engineers who design chips may soon be thrown out of work in the face of new technologies automating even their highly skilled professions.

What makes the entire venture more precarious is the degree to which the computer industry is subject to international competition. While American industries have always competed with their overseas counterparts, in the postwar years they had a jump on European and Japanese competition and soon dominated the world economy. They had time to develop large capital resources during the period needed to retool or develop new product lines. General Motors is still in business today in the face of more efficient Japanese manufacturers because it had the capital reserves needed to weather the losses of the mid-1970s. Much of the domestic electronics industry, outside of such well-entrenched stalwarts as IBM, lacks the capital to offset sharp competition from overseas rivals in the future. These companies are forced to trim their work forces quickly in response to market slumps or competitive disadvantages. Poor judgment in marketing strategies, research and development emphases, or pricing have immediate repercussions on thousands of people. A sense of responsibility for their employees' well-being is a concern that most of these companies lack. Under the guise of maintaining an entrepreneurial spirit, they have few policies for retraining or assessing the impact of their activities on local communities. It is the logic of the Wild West all over again, but this time instead of isolated boom towns and ghost towns the legacy could be a ruined industrial civilization.

# THREE

## Of Managers
## and Micros

"Real managers don't use terminals."

*Warren*
Manager

THERE WAS A TIME when office computers were tucked away in a climate-controlled, invariably windowless room. The computer room in those days was the exclusive preserve of a technical underclass far removed in function and prestige from the corporation's central command. Today, computers are moving from the back rooms to the corner offices. No longer viewed as primarily a "number-cruncher" for generating mailing lists and figuring payroll checks, the computer is becoming the corporate manager's trusted right hand and badge of modernity.

William Woodside, president of the American Can Company, has commented that the portfolios of future top executives "must include the ability to manage information" since information will be regarded as an asset like any other to be gathered and controlled. Computer literacy will be essential.

This isn't good news to everyone in the higher echelons. Executives and managers suffer from the same anxieties and fears about computerization as do those in the "employee subsystem." Many attribute their successful careers to their ability to make gut decisions, take risks, size up a colleague, drop and read hints, play office politics. They pride themselves on their shrewdness and intuition. Their lines of communication are informal and personal— the business lunch, the quick phone call. They don't see themselves as data processors.

John, a senior manager at an insurance company, is in his mid-fifties. Since computers have been introduced in the office, he has felt frustrated. The detailed new procedures for using the equipment irritate him, and he refuses to try them out. He behaves as if nothing has changed. He relies on his secretary, as always, to circulate memos and file notes. "I'm waiting for the companies to simplify it. Someday they'll have a machine I can talk to."

Executives may resist using computers because they simply don't want to handle a keyboard. Many of them don't know how to type, and are proud of it. The keyboard is traditionally a secretary's tool, and to many managers, a liberal sprinkling of computers in the management suites —with the implication that managers will have to learn to use (and type on) terminals—is an alarming proletarian trend. This is one reason that Apple designed Lisa, its higher-level business computer, with a hand-held cursor so that commands could be pointed to, not typed. The new Hewlett Packard 150, also designed for the executive, features touch rather than keyboard control, and appeals to the working style of its potential buyers.

The new computing power makes the office a faster-changing environment than before, with staff size and composition in flux. The job of a middle manager or supervisor is essential to observe other people's functions. But once a company goes on-line, these monitoring tasks can be consolidated or moved upstairs to the executive suite. The company's work goes on mostly within computers, and activity becomes more easily measured. Middle managers can suddenly seem overabundant. Most companies in the recent lean years have tended to lay off employees when they bring computers into the workplace. The pattern more and more is to let middle managers go while hiring lower-level staff to cover the seemingly irreducible clerical work. In the business world, one of the measures of power is the number of people one supervises. Managers often get an inkling of the future when they notice their span of control—the number of staffers reporting to them—shrinking. They sense themselves slipping on the corporate ladder and wonder if they'll be the next to go. The resulting stress is considerable.

Middle managers also know that with computers they spend less time monitoring and more time being monitored. With computerization, quarterly reports become monthly or even weekly reports; if an unsound decision is made or an unlucky risk taken, there is less time to fix it before the next report points it out.

Bureaucrats or supervisors who are not accustomed to being watched over feel nervous that their work is now subject to monitoring from above, or perhaps by peers. But while clerical workers have no say in whether management counts their keystrokes or times their phone calls, managers and executives may simply choose not to commit sensitive information to the computer. In January 1983, just before President Reagan praised high technology as the solution to the nation's economic problems, *Technology Review* published an article pointing out that the White House itself didn't use computers as a management tool. The reason was political: no one wanted to risk files accessible on the computer. Information, after all, is power. Why leave it temptingly within reach? In offices across the nation, workers feel threatened by the kind of access to information the computer allows.

Jack is a manager for a computer manufacturing company. When he comes across a discrepancy in inventory, he writes it down on a sheet of paper; he doesn't use his terminal. He wants to avoid having the problem traced to him. Other managers at his company do the same, he says.

Especially in transition periods, a manager is expected to lead by example. But when difficulties crop up in mastering a hardware or software system that is reputed to be "user friendly," the stress may be more keenly felt by the manager than by the general office worker. Even with the additional purchase of tutorials—software that guides the user through the parts of other software step by step—many managers begin to associate computers with frustration, not freedom or progress.

Ben, an educator with a Ph.D. from the University of

64

Chicago, is starting a business. He chose VisiCalc—a
financial spread-sheet software program widely touted as
easy to use—to prepare the budget. Four months later he
is still struggling to master the software. "This is like
going back to school. But it's a complete reversal," he
says. "At fifty, learning is supposed to be easier." The
frustration is doubly painful for Ben because of the widespread praise for the package. He feels humiliated, as if
something were suddenly wrong with him.

Still, most managers know well that computer technology is the new key to productivity, and they had best
learn to use it or be left behind. They also realize that their
employees must learn to use it as well if the company itself
is not to be left behind. For those in positions of power, the
urge to adapt is often internalized, not imposed from outside. They try to do well. They take to heart the goals of
the company. In order to maintain a healthy sense of self,
clerical workers, who may be suffering the tension and
discomfort of being squeezed into new and unfamiliar
roles by the new technology, may cope by dissassociating
their company's interests from their own. The manager
and the computer professional, on the other hand, find it
difficult to view the adaptation process as a matter distant
from their own desires and goals. Without that psychological distance, the conflicts they feel are more deeply felt.
Thus the manager and the professional, although they
believe themselves to be immune to the harsh effects of the
new technology, are in fact very much at risk. It is the
successful manager, executive, or professional who, in
striving to succeed, may begin to identify too closely with
the technology and behave in ways that mimic computer
logic. In addition to the frustrations of trying to integrate
the new technology into the workplace to increase productivity and profits, managers are often unaware of the
subtle changes the technology is causing within themselves. Their decision-making, managerial style, and personality are influenced by the new dependence on
computers.

Sally's situation reflects this. As the manager of a winery an important part of her job is arranging export deals. Recently, she bought a software package to help her figure out whether it would be profitable for the winery to begin exporting to a new territory. Hearing of an important upcoming deal with an importer, she dropped everything else to work with the computer, assuming it would enable her to meet her deadline for the deal. She had to reassign others to handle her work. However, the particular needs of her business did not conveniently fit the software package, and she found she had to take her work home in order to prepare for her meeting with the importer. Exhausted, she began to feel angry because suddenly she found herself unable to cope with her work, and feared she would lose the deal altogether.

Sally made a common mistake: she didn't give herself enough time to learn the new system. She considered herself a top manager, and with computer power she assumed she would be a super-manager. That assumption ignores one of the hard realities of the computer world: new solutions always bring new problems. Time saved by using packaged software instead of designing a program oneself can be eaten up later when one tries to solve unique problems with the mass-produced software.

Stan runs a car rental and leasing agency. Recently, the parent company sent him two personal computers with custom software to improve the efficiency of his operation. He soon found the software didn't allow for all the last-minute changes that are part of the business. A customer, for example, asked to trade an assigned car for an air-conditioned model after one day of a four-day rental. Stan spent all his time trying to figure out how to modify the original data in the computer to fit the particular and varied demands of his customers. "I finally had to choose among three things: going nuts, hiring a person to input data, or returning the machines." He returned the machines.

Peter, a senior buyer for a mid-sized shoe retail chain,

has also been frustrated in his attempts to use computers. He convinced his boss to buy a software package to calculate inventory—how many shoes were being sold each week, how long shoes were sitting on the shelves, how many remained, and so on. Peter reasoned that the package would save them time. He has discovered that it does save time in some areas, but that saving is offset by new work created in others. The software package, for example, does not allow for defective shoes that customers return; each time that happens, Peter is bogged down in fitting the details into the computerized scheme. His workload has unexpectedly increased.

Managers typically gauge their own degree of success by measuring their subordinates' productivity. This managerial tendency is nothing new, but is intensified by the computer, which offers the alluring promise of maximum productivity with minimum effort. The bind occurs when managers find out that maximum productivity is just another myth. The disappointment of unmet expectations becomes another source of technostress.

The ability to accomplish a task often creates the need to execute that task—often too frequently. The labor-saving computer can become the labor-making computer. Budget updates, inventory control, sales projections, and other data that were commonly and comfortably evaluated quarterly or monthly can now be done weekly or daily. A common mistake of companies that confuse data output with meaningful productivity is to believe that if computer power is good, more is better. So businesses buy a great number of computers capable of generating large amounts of data. Information pollution results—data everywhere, with little idea of what to do with it, except to keep processing, distributing, and analyzing it. Businesses are so taken by the idea that computers will advance the future of their companies that they often buy systems that they neither understand nor require. Many consultants to businesses are surprised when simpler or less expensive solutions are not welcomed; technological needs are assumed to warrant expensive, long-term solutions (the opposite of personnel needs, whose solutions are regarded as cheap and short-term), even though the turnover of outmoded technologies rivals that of employees. A personal computer with decentralized access, for instance, may be sufficient to handle the needs of a sales inventory staff, but the executive in charge may opt for a more complex minicomputer, with centralized access, because it seems more modern, more progressive, and heightens the department's image within the company.

68

Steven is a manager in the accounting department of a large city hospital that has recently implemented a database management system, administered by an outside service bureau. The goal of the system is to control costs. But there are so many variables and so much data involved, the hospital management has decided that the service bureau should produce updated weekly reports. Steven and many others now receive thick printouts every week listing details that reports hadn't kept track of before.

"What am I supposed to do?" Steven says. "It's costing us a fortune just to do the reports." He recently tried to remove his name from the mailing list but didn't have the right computer code to do so, which added to his frustration. He now puts the printouts in cardboard boxes when they arrive and stores them in the basement.

Managers are also subject to the physiological effects caused by the stress of computerized work environments. In a study entitled "Stress Reactions in Computerized Administrative Work" two Swedish psychologists discovered that white-collar personnel who worked with VDTs at a large insurance company in Stockholm had significant problems related to stress. In relation to control groups, the group using VDTs excreted more adrenaline, a stress hormone, under ordinary working conditions, and after work for a longer period of time. The temporary breakdown in the computer system produced marked elevation in blood pressure and adrenaline excretion.

For the manager, as for the clerical worker, a key

element of technostress is a distorted sense of time. Days, hours, and minutes take on new meaning as time is compressed and accelerated. Recognition of what is humanly possible fades. Jobs that took days before computerization are expected to be done in hours. Schedules are packed, putting strain on managers and staff alike. Software that was once appreciated for its speed, such as VisiCalc, is suddenly viewed as clumsy and slow.

For many managers, not only has the computer put more time into each second, but it has also packed more seconds into each workday. Executives on business trips or vacations can now use computers to stay intimately involved with the goings-on at the main office, reading reports and okaying decisions, instead of waiting until they return home. Some major hotel chains feature computers to attract business clientele. Business portables such as the Kaypro sell spectacularly not just because they are used to play video games at home, but because they extend the workday into the evening and the weekend. With a briefcase-micro and a phone link, the conscientious young executive-on-the-move who once brought a few files home in an attaché case can now bring *all* his files home— the whole office—complete with instant electronic access to the firm's central computer.

Within the business world, all this new technology is giving way to new corporate games. These games are part of a growing corporate culture; in essence they are strategies for survival. As computers are brought into the workplace, certain patterns of applying pressure and grabbing power are noticeable among managers. The early stages of computerization are periods of flux, and ambitious employees may see this time as a chance to strengthen their position within the company by using the technology to their advantage. There are at least three popular games, each with particular variations: the Star Game, the Ransom Game, and the Maintenance Game.

Jon is a typical player of the Star Game. A vice president in a Midwestern savings and loan company, he is clever and aggressive. There has never been any doubt in anyone's mind that he is on the company's fast track. Recently, Jon was sent to manage a distant new branch. Knowing that in order to climb the corporate ladder he must maintain his visibility, Jon almost immediately pushed for and got a new software package to handle large loans. Jon thus appeared modern and progressive even though he himself knew little about the old software and procedures.

The hands-on employees below Jon were unhappy about the change. Alice, a supervisor, was irritated that she was never consulted. She expected, in fact, that new federal regulations would limit the new software's usefulness. The vendor had claimed the software was a "labor saver," and Jon had bought it for visibility. Meanwhile, it had only been a year since the last new installation, and Alice knew her staff had only just begun to settle down and be comfortable with it.

Alice, to support Jon, had to lie to her employees by telling them the new software was essential. She felt miserable as a result, torn between company loyalty and personal honesty. The employees, for their part, openly kidded each other about who would get a promotion for bringing in the new system. They had witnessed the internal politics of software implementation before.

Managers increasingly use technology as a tool to maintain their own visibility or enhance their image within the company. Gary, for example, is the CEO (chief executive officer) of a mid-sized consumer products company. Having a clear idea of how his employees should enter the information age, he recently purchased five hundred IBM Personal Computers. Gary spent little time or effort consulting with others on the purchase, neither querying employees on how they might use the computers nor planning an implementation scheme. Nevertheless, among his peers in the business community Gary received instant recognition for his farsightedness.

Technology frequently serves the executive image, which some suspect is the reason IBM Personal Computers are so popular—executives associate IBM with power and success. Computers have taken over as prestige items. Executives were expected to spend more on computer gadgetry for Christmas gifts in 1983 than on alcohol or tickets to sporting events.

When computers are bought for the wrong reasons, companies as well as workers can suffer. The CEO of a large oil company in California bought one thousand personal computers for his engineers to keep them happy. A systems analyst for the company, when asked how implementation was going, replied, "I've got a horse and a cart, and I don't know how to hook them together. One guy even has two on his desk, one for financial projections and another that handles color graphics for his scientific work. It's a little hectic around here."

A variation of the Star Game occurs when middle managers, sensing the commitment their superiors have made to the technology, jump on the bandwagon. In order to appear equally committed, this group pushes deadlines for implementation and tolerates a minimum of interference—employee difficulties, for instance. One middle manager at a computer manufacturing company put it this way:

> It's my job around here to get things moving. . . . We installed a new computer-aided design system for the design group. It cost us a small fortune. It's simple: the faster we're up to speed, the sooner we get a return. You've got to push people, make them stretch, but you've got to be careful not to push them too far because they'll burn out. . . . The only people you don't need to worry about burning out are the grunts. There's plenty of them around.

In one high-tech firm that builds custom computer systems for industry, a systems analyst had taken great care to design a systems plan that would avoid bottlenecks and reduce rush times. The manager, his boss, praised the systems analyst lavishly for his efforts, but the analyst found out later that the manager had ignored his plans altogether and was pushing everyone to produce ahead of schedule. Some people adapted to the pressure, but others could not. Bottlenecks and rush times resulted as the synchronization between people was broken. The manager, when asked how he got his reputation as such a tough character, replied, "Actually, I'm sensitive to what they go through. But Jack [the president] isn't exactly an understanding guy. To stay in his favor, I have to produce."

The Ransom Game is another popular ritual of the computerized corporation. Historically, when skilled workers felt unduly pressured by management, they would slow the production of their special products as a form of protest. Management would undoubtedly notice, because management understood what was involved and how much time a job should take. Today, in workplaces where new technology is being brought in, projects are highly complex. Management often lacks a real understanding of how the implementation will change people's jobs and work flow. There are always unanticipated problems, and control over the project is often poorly worked out. How does one measure productivity, for example, if it's impossible to anticipate what workers will actually face in a project or how long it will take them to solve problems?

Industrial-era managers controlled production rates by simply keeping an eye on workers. For example, a manager could see when an industrial worker wasn't doing his job; he could see the worker walking around, daydreaming, or talking with others. Today, a programmer working on a software project may walk around frequently, lost in thought, trying to solve a problem, but that is more than likely a necessary part of the problem-solving process. Evaluating this worker's productivity is difficult. Companies have tried to institute productivity programs to get more out of technical workers. Instituting standards such as a minimum number of lines of programming per day is an example of an attempt to control production. The problem is that eight lines of program written to solve a complex problem may be as productive as fifteen lines written for rather perfunctory purposes. The only aspect of production the manager can observe is the outcome: whether workers get their jobs done and how fast they do them.

Ultimately, battle lines are drawn around time. When managers apply too much pressure, the professional staff rebels. Not in Luddite measures—smashing machines— but by subtly manipulating time. A project leader of a software application project put it this way:

> As soon as I feel management is pushing too hard for us to meet schedules, I make sure that we revise the time estimated to complete certain tasks. A lot of times management doesn't understand the work, and even if they do, they don't understand it well enough to know the problems we really face. If I can't slow down the project, the next project gets double the time I'd estimate is really needed.

Such schedule-adjusting is commonplace. A programmer employed by a large clothing manufacturer commented:

> Every time I see the consultants come in the door, I have to laugh. The productivity boys, as I call them, try to get us to produce a lot of code every day. Code in, code out. The only thing they don't realize is that producing code is not like making widgets. There's a lot more to it. . . . Ultimately, they have to come to me to get me to do the work.

•

Time will be the prize over which struggles of the future will be waged. And to win that struggle, professional groups will have to hold their companies up for ransom. This can be the price for psychological integrity in current environments.

When new technology is introduced, professionals are often anxious about the decline of their own importance in the company. This fear, often ultimately a fear of losing one's job altogether, shows up in a number of covert ways. People in such positions can find themselves playing the Maintenance Game.

Kathy, a supervisor in a large urban bank, worried when a new computer program took over many of her duties in monitoring employees' work flow. The program not only broke down tasks into smaller work units, but also kept a record of each worker's performance. Kathy decided to learn as much as she could as fast as she could about the program. Then she gradually began making alterations in it so that she would continue to be vital to ongoing operations. When the manufacturer of the program asked her to refrain from making changes until the system's expected bugs were worked out, she replied, "The program is *full* of bugs. Without me constantly tampering with it, nothing would get done around here."

Another case of the Maintenance Game occurred in a computer-parts warehouse. Bob, the warehouse manager, was in constant battle with a software company that made turn-key inventory systems for tracking everything from changing costs to daily parts inventories. (Turn-key systems are installed ready to operate, unlike customized systems, which are built to order.) These systems, when they need altering, are supposed to be left alone for at least the first six months so that patterns of problems can be analyzed. Bob, who had spent years learning the idiosyncrasies of the parts-inventory business, had this to say about his company's new system:

> No one can take all of what I know [about inventory] and put it into a program. . . . The system has been one big headache. I'm constantly having to change it to account for what is really going on around here. I've had to work on it since the day it was installed.

Asked if he followed the suggestions of the manufacturer to let time pass before tampering with the system, and then not to make alterations alone, Bob answered that that was a senseless approach to the problem: the software's designers knew less than he did and the software company was just trying to make money on alterations. The president of the software company, which has been making this turn-key inventory system for ten years, was asked about the situation. He suggested a different explanation:

> The real problem is that the CEO [of the parts company] won't see to it that his people are supported. They're all afraid that they'll be replaced, or they're not really sure what will happen to them. It [the software complaint] has nothing to do with the system itself. Without followup from the CEO, the system is doomed.

The Maintenance Game is the high-tech version of a familiar attitude about technology, the attitude typified by suggestions like "wait till Frank gets back from lunch—he knows how to fix the copier." It is Frank's knowledge that makes the copier run. Frank isn't just another piece of information in the system; he is special. He is needed for its operation. This need affords a degree of security in a world run increasingly on algorithms. It is not surprising that maintenance costs run approximately 35 percent of system costs. No one has yet studied how much of these costs are due to actual system failures and how much to corporate games. It is a question worth asking.

\*　　\*　　\*

75

Technostress, as we have seen in Chapter 2, similarly affects everyone who works closely with computers. For accountants, engineers, lawyers, teachers, writers, and of course computer experts such as programmers and systems analysts, machine-dependence is creating a complex of pressures and temptations.

The quantification of mental work is creeping up the job ladder to those disciplines that have always required a high level of abstract thinking. This trend remains largely unnoticed, which adds significantly to the problem. Paul, for example, works for a large architectural firm. He prides himself on being an artist who works creatively with space. Not long ago, in order to increase work quality and speed, his firm purchased a CAD (computer-aided design) system. The architects now use electronic styluses to produce drawings directly on the screens of their computer terminals; the architects mark the endpoints of a line or the corners of a room, and the design program draws the rest. Paul finds he can't concentrate on his work, and the rate at which he produces finished drawings has slacked off. He secretly fears that his identity as an artist is threatened, and has unsettling dreams in which he pictures himself plugged into a machine working on an assembly line.

Creative, problem-solving workers often get their best ideas when they have time to mull things over. With project times monitored more closely than ever before, the time needed for such mental processes as intuition is undervalued or ignored.

As work multiplies and the time expected for completion shrinks, the result is technostress. As we know from psychological studies, excessive stress fosters rigidity in problem-solving. The solutions that result are less likely to reflect creative thinking. Thus the emphasis on productivity that accompanies computerization results in less (and less effective) output.

Speeding up one's work, or trying to, alters the way one thinks. A writer using a word processor can work faster than a writer using a typewriter. However, many writers using word procesors report that the newfound speed alters the relation between conceiving an idea and phrasing it on paper. The change causes some writers to write in a sparer style, using shorter sentences and simpler grammar. Some readers find the result pleasing; others find it telegramlike. Magazine editors have commented that writers using word processors, when asked to rewrite stories, have an unhealthy tendency to think of their writing in modular terms; they are less likely to view the initial effort as a first draft to be set aside while a second draft is "run through the typewriter," and more likely to view it as a modifiable entity from which offending sentences or blocks of type can be deleted and to which new ones are seamlessly inserted. The new versions are often inadequate.

The speed-up of work does more than undercut work quality. When people spend less time on creative work and problem-solving and more on machine manipulation, they often end up feeling less challenged by their work. Without mental stimulation, no job can feel rewarding. This is a phenomenon efficiency experts invariably miss.

Jane graduated from a contemporary-minded architectural school in 1982. She avoided using computers there, although they were plentiful, and prides herself on her creativity and sense of aesthetics. She succeeded in being hired by a prestigious architectural firm. Her first job was to design a small part of a larger building project —a parking lot—and her supervisor has given her a software package to deal with all the client's requirements. She never visited the site; the information she needed was brought to her, and she typed it into the computer. She became upset and shocked, wondering if her education was a waste, and her career choice a mistake.

Few professionals feel this bind more keenly than the computer experts themselves—the programmers and systems designers and analysts.

Mark, a computer engineer for an electronics firm in

Silicon Valley whose specialty is circuitry design, loved computer work as a discipline, but when asked what he most wanted out of his particular job, he answered without hesitation, "Challenge." His job is not exciting; it's too routine, and he despises routine.

Unlike the clerical worker, or even other professionals, the computer professional is expected to be analytical. But all share a similar source of stress: understimulation. All need the opportunity to use their own judgment, follow hunches, and try out new ideas.

It is evident that in the professional ranks, as in the business world generally, the way work is being structured can easily defeat people who want to do quality work. A manager from an electronics firm said, "We don't want engineers to waste time evaluating the software they use. We'll hire others to do that." The engineer's job thus becomes less creative and he or she feels less responsible for it. In aerodynamics, for example, the engineer is presented with a program that models the behavior of an airplane inside a wind tunnel; the engineer enters variables describing the aircraft, and the program calculates its behavior. However, the engineer has no way of knowing whether or not the simulation is accurate. The assumptions that went into designing the program are not shared with its user. Some engineers may be relieved that they don't have to worry about such details, but opportunities for innovation are growing increasingly scarcer.

Sam is a soil engineer. His job is to analyze such factors as soil composition, slope, and rainfall to determine whether a particular site is suitable for a planned building. Recently he bought a software package that would allow him simply to plug in the variables. But after thinking about it, he didn't know whether to trust the program. "I didn't know who put it together and whether they worked out all the relationships right." Sam is uneasy because the matter of trust is an important issue for a professional. Trusting a "black box" seems to him a shirking of his duties as an engineer. What happens if a building he ap-

78

proves collapses? Sam has sought out the authors of the package and questioned them several times about their assumptions. He has realized, with regret, that he has saved himself neither time nor money.

We must question how the next generation of professionals will derive the hands-on experience, the tactile and visual perceptions of the materials they work with, that will insure innovation, experimentation, and new dimensions.

The distinction between the expert and the user is becoming a finer one. Programmers see productivity quotas applied to their work—so many lines of code per day are expected from each employee. They are treated more and more as production staff, not specialists. The carpenters of computer programs are being replaced by the prefab builders.

Henry manages the data-processing department of a bank. In his fifties now, he spent years coming up through the ranks, including twelve years as a senior programmer. "One thing that makes me sad," he says, "is that the bank is sending kids to learn programming for several months, and they come back and they don't really know how to program. They write sloppy code. Programming used to be an art, it took years to learn, but not anymore. It costs companies too much money."

Thanks to the popularity of canned programs for businesses, the role of in-house programmers is changing. They are more likely to add modular components to already existing programs than to create new ones. More time is spent fixing others' work than solving problems creatively. Large companies, due to the proliferation of software, have begun to build information resource centers. The staff of these centers are called librarians but they are really specialized file clerks. With the amount of specialized software commercially available, firms no longer need their own staff to keep things running. The upshot among the computer experts is a sense that they, too, are losing control over their work—just when it looked like the computer revolution was going to make their lives secure.

As managers and professional workers become machine-dependent, their social skills and interests also atrophy. They spend less time chatting with visitors and phone callers, and they resist attending staff meetings. The CAD-equipped architect, for example, soon becomes accustomed to data brought in from outside, manipulated on the VDT, and printed out. The procedure seems beautifully self-contained. The computer becomes the focal point of all productive activity.

Stan, an office manager in an oil company, does much of his work on a computer in his office. "I can't understand why people want to go to meetings," he says. "With my terminal I've got access to all the information I want."

Staff meetings may not be the most productive human endeavor known, but without contact with one's fellow workers and employees, working relations become distant and formalized. For both the manager and the professional, social isolation can be very harmful. Every hour spent communing with a computer is an hour spent living in the machine's world, a universe of codes and procedures. Those who work at home with computers feel this most keenly.

Helen, the sales manager of a computer company, gave birth to her first child last year. The company encouraged her to extend her maternity leave and continue working at home, giving her a personal computer and a modem for electronic mail. "At first, I'd just hop out of bed—I couldn't wait to log on and check for mail." Six months later, her feelings had changed: "I wanted to go back. I was surprised—I really missed the people I worked with."

People still communicate while at the computer, via electronic mail and in-house message systems, but they don't chat; they "log on."

Carl, a business consultant who does a great deal of writing, began working with an outside typist last year.

He would drive the three miles to her house to pick up material that she had typed, and they would always sit and talk. Often she would give him ideas or make suggestions. Carl recalls, "She would say, 'You missed a point' or 'This isn't very clear. . . .' One day a few months ago, she called and said, 'You don't have to come over here anymore. I'm getting an Apple and a modem. You use yours and send me stuff by phone.' I actually felt distressed. There isn't the same back-and-forth anymore."

When electronic communication becomes a substitute for speech, eye contact, and body language, it is a depersonalizing influence. Already, it is breaking down social customs and graces that were once considered a necessary part of being civilized. Like the computer users who "flame" (send obscene messages), managers are blunt when the medium is electronic. One sales manager for a Los Angeles firm noticed that managers treated underlings more curtly when communicating by computer: "They would say things . . . they wouldn't have said face to face." Even in its mildest form, electronic communication is robbing us of the chance to humanize business transactions.

We live in a corporate culture sensitized to hints of favor and rebuke. We pay careful attention to the size of our office and the view from our window. Since the 1960s the trend in work relations has been toward the let's-communicate approach ("What I hear you saying is...."). Into this culture comes the impersonality of machine communication, and the rules change. It's easier to be curt, insensitive to others, or even nasty. The refinements in business etiquette that developed in order to help people work closely together are fading with the increasing isolation of the worker.

For some, under these conditions, the inner drive to achieve and excel threatens to culminate in a computer-human symbiosis. The computer is no longer a force that inspires anxiety, fear, or resistance, even subconsciously. It is at this point that an individual risks becoming techno-centered, and suffering the most serious symptom of tech-nostress—total identification with a machine.

Still, proponents abound. John Naisbitt, in his widely read book, *Megatrends,* talks in glowing terms of the fantastic potential of computers to extend our senses and our sensitivity. Unfortunately, although his "high-tech/high-touch" imagery appeals to us, the reality is just the reverse. The computer world is symbol-intensive, not sensual, and constricts our abilities to interpret and create in a manner that reflects our unique human sensibilities.

The concept of progress is so interwoven with our feelings about the computer that questioning its impact on the quality of work and thinking is usually viewed as heresy. And yet this is the essential question. Increasingly, because of the advanced knowledge needed to solve complex problems, companies and their personnel will need to distinguish themselves by their open-minded, creative, and wide-ranging approaches to problems. Thinking, on the professional level, should take more time, not less. What we are facing is the mechanization of the mind, an inner transformation that we must hope will not continue in the direction of the factory model. If it does, we will lose the most valuable frontier we have: our inner selves and the quality of our thinking.

82

# FOUR

## Robot/Human— Human/Robot

"I don't think the mind was made to do logical operations all day long."

*Patrice*
Engineer

HUMAN NATURE is not fixed. We do not blindly follow the behavioral patterns of a species, the way birds roost and moles burrow. We are the only animal that must forge its own way of living. In essence, we create ourselves. Where animals have an existence, humans have a life—we reflect, we examine and reexamine, we set goals and enunciate principles. We are historical by nature: we learn how to behave not only by imitation and by trial and error but also from what our elders tell us, from what we hear and read about the past, and what we deduce from experience. We have as much capacity for truth as we do for illusion.

Because we are not substantially ruled by instinct, we develop what psychologists call character. Erich Fromm, in *The Anatomy of Human Destructiveness*, defines character as "the relatively permanent system of all noninstinctual strivings through which man relates himself to the human and natural world." Character is, in a sense, man's second nature. Differences in character are due in part to differences in social and technical conditions. A person who lives in a place where goods are bartered acquires a temperament and view of the world different from that of a person who works for pay in electronic space.

It would be a mistake, however, to think that an individual's character is entirely a product of the environment. As Fromm is careful to point out, all people have in common their organic drives—hunger and sex—and their existential needs—the need for love and companionship, a sense of belonging, and for values like truth and beauty. The fulfillment of these needs is crucial to a person's psychological health, just as the fulfillment of organic drives is necessary for survival. In striving to attend to these drives and needs, the individual behaves in a way that is consistent with a fundamental humanness.

Human character has to a large extent been shaped by technology. Lewis Mumford, in *Technics and Civilization,* carefully traced the influence of the machine on people's lives throughout major periods in Western civilization. Mumford was most interested in demonstrating that before the new industrial processes could take hold on a broad scale, a reorientation of wishes, habits, ideas, and goals was necessary. He emphasized that "what is usually called the industrial revolution, the series of industrial changes that began in the eighteenth century, was a transformation that took place in the course of a much longer march." The transformation of the human character by the machine, according to Mumford, began as early as the tenth century, when the clock first began to encourage people to perceive their lives as a sequence of measurable events regulated by schedules. As civilization evolved, the machine contributed to a more "objective personality," in Mumford's words. This personality was one that valued order, neutral observation, and counting. It is readily apparent how different people of the medieval world were from people today, the former with their belief that God provided order in the world, the latter with their faith in technological solutions and explanations. This basic tenet shapes the way people view themselves and others and even the way they lead their daily lives.

Mumford was disturbed not by the development of the machine nor by its influence on human character per se, but by the inability of people to assimilate it properly and thus free themselves to move beyond it. Mumford interjected a note of caution: "Until we have absorbed the lessons of objectivity, impersonality, neutrality, the lessons of the mechanical realm, we cannot go further in our development toward the more richly organic, the more profoundly human."

85

Mumford was examining evolution of the human character over periods of centuries. It took a thousand years for humanity to incorporate the lessons of the machine in its psyche. It took an era for humanists to call our attention to some of the new problems this posed. With the acceleration of technical innovation, we can no longer afford to wait for the luxury of hindsight. Technostress has already become a dangerous reality, and we must learn to come to grips with it now.

Jacques Ellul, in *The Technological Society*, has pointed out that the impact of new technology on our collective psyche is more forceful now than during the industrial era. Not only has it become a true environment, a ubiquitous part of our lives requiring mastery for survival, but it has a power of its own. Machines have become so interconnected that one device necessitates another, which in turn generates the need for more machines and newer applications to keep pace with the trend. For instance, a computer used for selecting fabrics in a store is connected to a computer in the stock room that is linked to a computer in a distribution center that could ultimately be hooked up to a terminal in a textile factory. More computers mean more computer systems and more computer procedures. According to Ellul, human character is bound by the computer. We find ourselves confused, overwhelmed, and culturally at sea. Our ability to exercise free choice and pursue meaningful lives is made difficult, if not impossible.

Questions of values and free choice—existential needs, in Fromm's words—are being explored within the computer community itself. Joseph Weizenbaum, professor of computer science at the Massachusetts Institute of Technology, has written extensively on how the role advocated for the computer by many social scientists and computer intellectuals intensifies problems of alienation. Weizenbaum maintains that the espoused benefits of the "information society" are in fact questionable. Overreliance on the computer, in his view, is undercutting people's ability to perceive and evaluate their own lives; instead, the computer reinforces "a kind of pragmatic positivism bordering on scientism." This approach to the world, a hyper form of counting logic, may ultimately reduce people's ability to think creatively by not allowing them to see alternatives to their existing problems. Weizenbaum fears that as people model themselves on the computer, their self-images as dynamic, feeling beings will be eclipsed by the image of the computer as the universal hero.

Although there is no fixed bundle of characteristics    87
we can refer to as human nature, there is a point beyond which we become nonhuman. This is the point at which we no longer strive to realize our potential to become feeling, sentient beings. The elegance of being human is reflected in our gift of being able to articulate the finest shades of meaning and feeling. Most of us have an inner desire to blossom, to be creative, to expand our horizons and our bonds with others. When we make an all-out effort to adapt to new technology and to become, in effect, high-performance machines ourselves, we frustrate those inner strivings. In so doing, we stunt our most valuable human qualities. In recalling those experiences in life we all most prize—occasions when we express strong emotions, appreciate a beautiful work of art, share a touching moment —the force of those experiences leaves us no room to doubt that we are people, not machines. The central question that we must try to face is this: given our tremendous potential as human beings, how well are we living up to our promise? It is claimed that the computer is the greatest extension of human experience and culture thus far—a tool to do our bidding—but this does not fit the experience of how our use of computers is affecting our culture.

Most warnings about technology's effect on human character have been couched in general, societal terms. Social critics have tended not to venture from the speculative to the concrete by examining the individual lives of people for whom the computer is their culture. This broad-brush approach is highly useful, but it is incomplete. As

Arthur Koestler once commented, "Facts don't bleed. People do." The computer has spread so extensively in so short a time that already evidence of how people's characters are being transformed is all around us. In some cases the change is subtle; in others it is dramatic. The latter cases—instances where people have become technocentered—help illuminate what threatens to become the normal behavior of our time.

Joann is a computer manager for a large urban bank. She is an expert computer programmer and spends most of her time designing new systems for the bank to use. She feels comfortable in her job and challenged by her work. She hates meetings, wants to be left alone at work, and experiences her co-workers as an unnecessary burden. She sometimes neglects her personal appearance. When she returns home at the end of the day, she communicates to her husband in a yes-no fashion and soon retreats to her room where she can have peace and quiet.

Joann exhibits the classic behavior of the technocentered individual. Her relationship to the computer is determining her relationship to all else, and the computer comes first. She has reordered her priorities, and from her perspective it probably appears to be a good arrangement. She thinks of herself as successful and well-adjusted, and only friction with her family may force her to see the harm this has done to her personality.

Highly motivated computer users, like any other achievement-oriented workers, have a strong desire to excel. They want to master their work, expand their abilities, and feel challenged. They cannot tolerate loose ends, sloppy organization, undefined goals. They see themselves as plowing through a succession of problems and leaving a steady trail of completed tasks behind them. This outlook pushes them in the direction of control, because control engenders task completion.

Maladaptation of this kind is not simply the result of character flaws. Our entire culture is pushing people in the direction of computer-compatibility. People do not gener-

88

ally learn to master the computer for the same reasons they master the violin. The majority of computer users are forced to learn the technology, directly or indirectly: directly, through fear of losing one's job, or indirectly, through an awareness that career success and advancement hinge on computer skills. Companies expect high performance from their work force just as they do from their machines, and ambitious people must learn to meet the high standards of electronic space or move aside.

Adaptation to intense computer work is a complex phenomenon. Computer literacy, which once referred to an ability to use software and do a little programming in BASIC, has broadened. It now often means familiarity with several computer languages and systems and, by extension, enough ease with the technology to use it to expand one's own abilities. For the achiever, there is continual pressure to stay on top of the technology, since it is constantly evolving as new products appear, change, and disappear. There are no niches to slip into and relax.

Pressure on the computer worker can be enormous. When large companies computerize, slipups can be disastrous: the smallest error can disrupt a delivery schedule or misplace millions of dollars.

Jack is a senior programmer for a large bank. When a new system goes on line, he spends his night in a motel near the bank, so that if problems develop he is nearby to come fix them. Every night for weeks afterwards, even when he sleeps undisturbed, he dreams that he's received the dreaded phone call—"It blew up!"—and must jump out of bed to get the system running again before the entire staff comes in to use it.

Harrowing or not, many computer workers thrive on this sort of pressure. Challenge is often the stimulus that motivates them. Attracted by the possibility to do jobs faster and better, they push themselves, moving from competence to excellence. Completing a predetermined task is no longer the real goal; designing more difficult tasks and mastering them is. To create the challenges they need, users keep improving upon already workable solutions—writing more elegant code, shortening a procedure —so that the tasks at hand keep expanding to fit the available time. As a result, deadlines are always imminent. The computer workers in this case have a high degree of personal involvement in the work they are doing. Their nervous systems are extremely attuned to minute fluctuations in the work system. The smallest glitch can ruin an entire day. Boundaries between the self and the world of the machine become dangerously fuzzy.

With the new mastery of information and problem-solving skills, mental workloads become heavier. Microdecision-making—the incessant choices that must be made when a complex task is handled as a sequence of subroutines—adds to the burden.

At forty-two, James is a systems analyst at a manufacturing company, An ace analyst, he is a worker with few peers and one who, because few others understand what goes into the job, earns little praise. Since at each job only he understands the various programs, he feels constantly badgered to clarify them to co-workers. He explains, "I feel as though more and more information is demanded of me." Large chunks of his time and energy are drained. This is his fourth employer in ten years. Each time James quits a job, he feels an intense freedom, a tremendous sense of release that lasts until his knowledge catches up with him at another job. He is, ironically, a victim of his own expertise.

Users may begin to feel tired and find they cannot calculate as quickly, plan as well, or make decisions as carefully as before. Mental engagement is high-pitched, concentration intensely focused. The person is immersed in processing information, which overshadows normal sensory awareness. Users may start to lose track of time—a morning spent on a problem can seem like no time at all. Meals are skipped and meetings missed as a problem is pursued. But symptoms of an overtaxed mind are not as easily recognized as those of an overtaxed body, so hard-working computer users bend their minds to questionable limits.

Shelley is a senior systems analyst in her thirties who designs computer-related jobs for a large company which includes diagramming responsibilities and calculating work flow. She has to think in a precise and orderly fashion. She is aware that the job is making tremendous mental demands on her, and when she leaves work she needs a long time to disengage from her "work mode" of thinking. To make the transition, she takes a shower, which helps to tell her she is home. "But that doesn't always work," she says. She cannot always make the break between work life and home life. Shelley has a four-year-old child, and she has begun to worry that her job has affected her abilities as a mother. "Being a mother is about interruptions," she says, "and being a good mother is being able to handle them. Right now, I just can't tolerate interruptions."

Computer workers like Shelley are not yet technocentered—they are still capable of feelings—but they are on the threshold of becoming emotionally distant, a preliminary symptom of technostress. By contrast, psychologically healthy workers maintain a balanced relationship with whatever technology they use. They are able to be highly involved in their work without losing their own sense of self. When the pressure is on, they can maintain an integrity of personality by paying attention to their own limits, staying in touch with others, and looking for ways to integrate their work with their personal lives. They remain sensitive to the world and open to the challenges of new experiences. Newness refreshes and deepens them; it does not simply overwhelm or overstimulate them. Most of all, they maintain the capacity for insight—an emotional and intellectual understanding of themselves. Psychologically healthy workers will try to adapt the environment to their needs, not simply adapt themselves to their environment.

But working with computers is a potent activity. Overidentification with the machine can cause an unhealthy relation to one's work, crippling the psychological bases of insight. People in a pre-technocentered state begin to lose perspective; sometimes a pivotal point is reached when they realize that work is becoming all-encompassing, that they are "not themselves." At this point they may decide to try to come to grips with the situation, acknowledging their personal problems. A realization like this does not come easily. Yet without it, these people continue as before and, driven by the desire to excel, slip ever closer to a machinelike ideal. A human-oriented view of the world disappears and is replaced by a technology-oriented view.

92

Technocentered people push themselves in a constant effort to improve their work performance. They ignore their own limits. Mental fatigue sets in, and with it increasingly rigid thinking, less creative solutions, an unconscious slowdown in work rate, and a higher number of errors. Technocentered workers pattern their behavior after the technology. They don't take breaks, they don't talk about nonwork subjects, they don't think abstractly, and above all they don't question the reason for doing the job they're doing. The greater the fit between them and the technology, the less energy is wasted in struggling to improve performance. Technocentered people are trapped on a treadmill, although they lack the insight and the self-awareness to understand this. In the process, they sacrifice a feeling grasp of the real world. All that exists outside logical processes seems fuzzy to them.

Scott is an electrical engineer who does computer programming as part of his job. He must use mathematical equations to calculate the most efficient layouts for detailed electrical circuits. He describes his work as a vortex. At home at night—to his wife's distress—he finds himself lost in the equations fixed in his head, his mind going over and over a certain sequence, tracing the endless connections between numbers. It is a problem he knows he feels compelled to solve but cannot. Night after night, at home, his mind makes its logical loops.

The desire for technical mastery and the absence of social contact reinforce each other. Like a psychological defense, the technocentered person's relations with the outside world remain within safe bounds because the same behavior patterns are repeated again and again. Nothing new is experienced. Little is unpredictable. These people resemble a broken record played over and over. Freud, in referring to neurotics, called this sort of closed behavior the repetition compulsion: repeating past experiences and continually failing. Similarly, technocentered individuals are condemned to repeat a present with which they over-identify.

Where technoanxious people experience a sense of accelerated time, technocentered individuals lose all track of it. Hours and minutes are irrelevant as the task at hand consumes consciousness. Natural limits intrude upon them—their workday ends, they eat dinner, they go to sleep—but these seem only irritating discontinuities.

Where staff meetings may be unwelcome interruptions to adapting technical employees, they are intolerable interference to technocentered workers, who feel that meetings detract from their mission to generate code and work intensely with a program.

Jerry is a programmer working on a financial package for a software company. He has always found staff meetings and socializing with co-workers to be an annoyance, but lately he has become angered by any interruption in his work, no matter how trivial. "It's like making love," he says of programming. "If you were making love, you wouldn't want to be interrupted."

Bill, a team leader and lead programmer for IBM, comments, "I hate meetings," he says. "I suffocate at meetings. They're a complete waste of time."

Technocentered individuals operate in terms of perfection, sequential thinking, logic. Their entire cognitive structure is geared to the computer. Ambiguity and nuance are concepts the technocentered mind cannot "process." Communication must be efficient. Abbreviated language appeals to them because it accelerates communication. They weave acronyms and technical shorthand into their speech as much as possible. They prefer to communicate with people who are "system literate" so as to transfer information quickly, not interact. People who talk slowly or in general terms are avoided or ignored.

In the early stages of this syndrome, human relationships are a slight irritation. At work, friendships are superficial. Socializing is a vexing intrusion on work at the terminal. At home, excuses start. "One more line of program is all I have." "Sorry for not paying attention, I was thinking about work." Unfinished tasks dominate their private thoughts. Given a choice, they prefer to be left alone.

In full bloom, the condition leaves no room for excuses. At home, "I'll be through in a minute" becomes "Don't you understand what I'm doing?" At work, tenuous human alliances fade. The most minor interruptions are not merely irritations, they are a major source of stress. For the technocentered person—flat, without affect —it is the friction of social relations, not machine relations, that can provoke outbursts of anger. Such outbursts, however, are not so much manifestations of deep-seated hostility as they are mechanisms to ward off interference. For the technocentered worker, only productivity matters; unstructured, unfocused, or irrelevant activity has no redeeming value.

Instead of friendships, technocentered people satisfy what need for social contact they still have by superficial conversations. They have acquaintances, not friends, and the acquaintances are mostly those with whom they can talk shop. Genuine friendships require commitment and energy, and there is little time for either. Talking about nontechnological subjects is an exhausting effort.

Robert is a scientist for a high-tech company. He depends on a computer system daily to sort, analyze, and model many of his hunches about chemical processes. He is enthusiastic about his work and often works overtime. Lately, he has been irritated by things being out of place at home and annoyed by what he perceives to be his wife's slow thinking. He is unsettled when she uses too many words to express herself clearly, or when she tells a story. He is angry, generally, because she does not conform to his standards of perfect performance. He takes work home now in the evening so he can be left alone.

For technocentered people, the desire to conquer the system becomes greater than the desire for human rela-     95
tionships and human pleasures. The process of computer operation itself becomes pleasurable. The heightened stimulation of solving problems within a decision tree or making decisions several times a minute is a motivating force all its own. This mental engagement can be as excit-ing as sexual arousal, and makes the habit that much harder to break.

Adding to the stubbornness of the condition is the fact that these people are blind to their own predicament. The push for immediacy, the concentration on present problems only, weakens their ties with past experiences and thus their ability to reflect on their lives. Their memo-ries stretch only to the most recent events. For technocen-tered people, memory becomes "access to past events," an access limited by "search procedures" and "schemes for selected perception." Increasingly, they will respond, when pressed for additional or more in-depth information, "I haven't got access to that." This is not defensiveness, merely a determination that there is insufficient informa-tion available to make a reply. Memory, from this perspec-tive, is only recall. The healing power of memory is undermined. Technocentered people forget they once were different.

To the casual observer, technocentered people may seem to be the computer age's version of the obsessive-compulsive, the character type often associated with workaholics. Technocentered people certainly resemble obsessive-compulsives, but the differences are significant.

Both groups have trouble managing time and working within normal schedules. They lose themselves in detail, and cannot abide disorder or loose ends. Along with their intense powers of concentration, a fear of losing control is evident. Neither type is capable of appreciating and enjoying the non-work-related experiences of everyday living, although the obsessive-compulsive person can be warm and affectionate.

Obsessive-compulsives in general have an over-developed sense of volition, a belief that the world is what they make of it, that willpower shapes all. This leads to both intellectual and emotional rigidity; they sometimes seem to be trying to control and redirect *all* their emotions and desires. The result is a peculiar kind of self-awareness, as though an internal overseer were constantly issuing commands. Obsessive-compulsives often fall into role-playing, even going so far as to control the details of their facial expressions and ways of speaking. Compared to other neurotics, they are detached and self-critical; guilty consciences, self-doubt, and worry are common. Conflict haunts them.

Technocentered people, by contrast, feel no inner conflict. Where obsessive-compulsives carry out their jobs, whether doctor, lawyer, or secretary, "as if" committed to them, technocentered people, whose work is with computers, *are* their jobs. Where obsessives are preoccupied with self-doubt, technocentered people are not. They have no nagging sense that something psychological is wrong. They feel pressured, but they experience this as a desire to excel, to match the perfection of the machine. This absence of conflict is obvious when they talk about their work. Where the "overseer" within obsessives drives them to perform work they "should" do, technocentered people never feel forced to do their work. They are attached to it. Their needs and the demands of the system seem one and the same.

Obsessives harbor a latent hostility. They bristle when criticized. They present an appearance of hardness, of being "uptight." Technocentered people, by contrast, effect a waxen expressionlessness. They accept criticism as data to be processed; hostility is too exhausting and irrelevant. Much of computer work, in fact, requires that workers listen to and accept critical suggestions aimed at improving their end product.

A keen sense of personal guilt drives obsessives, who, whether at work or at home, always feel they are not doing quite as they should, which pushes them into acting out even more assiduously their various roles. Technocentered individuals live without guilt. They lack altogether a feeling for other people that is a precondition of guilt. Without guilt, they can easily dismiss appeals from others to change.

The motivation to change is also quite different for the two personalities. Obsessive-compulsives have a high tolerance for suffering, but nevertheless, they do not lose their ability to suffer. This is a crucial factor, because even an incomplete awareness of suffering can serve as a stimulus for change. Obsessives may be pushed to change by a feeling that their lives lack meaning, that their relationships are less than satisfying, or that they are not as creative in their work as they would like to be.

Technocentered people are only dimly aware of suffering, if at all. They may freely concede that work is stressful or that they are not pleasant to be with, but they accept that as the way things are. If adjustments are needed, they assume others can make them. They see themselves as successful, even happy. For a breakthrough to occur, an outside crisis is necessary, such as a spouse threatening to leave.

The obsessive-compulsive is a classic neurotic personality type, molded by experiences and relationships from early in life. Obsessives bring their bag of neuroses to any activity and any job—stocking shelves, playing softball, managing a company—and turn it into a pressure-filled experience. The personality shapes the work.

The technocentered person is a creation of technology. Victims may once have been sociable, relaxed, and caring, and after leaving their computer jobs, they soon become so again. The problem is not rooted in deep-seated neuroses. The work has determined the personality.

Some of the attributes of the obsessive-compulsive are greatly valued in today's society, shaped by the Protestant work ethic. Erich Fromm has observed that the obsessive-compulsive is the norm of industrial culture. We admire people who succeed in high-pressure jobs; the self-motivated, hard-charging young executive-on-the-move is a glamorous and envied model. But computer work invites a dangerous transformation of these qualities. Achievers may bring to any job the desire to perform well, but if the nature of that job is not based on a perfect machinelike ideal, any obsessive-type characteristics are softened and the workers retain their basic humanity. The special demands of working with computers exacerbate those obsessive-compulsive qualities without allowing for humanizing influences, such as ample social contact with other workers or a relaxed and informal milieu. The overspecialized character that results from high performance in technical work is destined to become the norm of electronic culture.

For the overspecialized character, accelerated performance becomes the overriding goal, supported by a logical world view that values what is fast and efficient. For the overspecialized character, psychological health is equated with correct solutions to problems, arrived at on schedule. Emotions are downplayed in the interest of achievement.

To understand this evolving character type, it is necessary to cite Freud's classic formulation of the human psyche and to examine how the dynamics of personality have changed since his time. To Freud, the infant was instinctive by nature. It was driven by lust, by which Freud meant satisfaction of basic drives such as hunger.

98

Freud theorized that pleasure thus had survival value. The psychological life of the child was ruled by what Freud called the id, motivated by the "pleasure principle."

The child, however, faced a most difficult reality. There were struggles with paternal authority, taboos against pleasures of the body, and often a scarcity of love. In order to survive, the child had to learn to renounce instinct, obey social rules, and respect authority. In doing so, the child formulated the ego. Using a mechanism Freud called repression, the child internalized conflict between the id and the ego and created the superego, which controls the impulses of the id so that the child can conform to the requirements of the social order. Only in this way could the child ever be socialized to function in the world outside the family—specifically, the world of work. The sensuous child had to become the productive adult.

99

Freud's theory, while it accurately accounts for repression caused by the reality principle, has become dated; it fails to take into account the fact that the "reality principle"—the interplay between id, ego, and superego—changes as a culture changes. For Freud, the psyche was defined by internal tensions, arrayed within an assumed set of family relationships. These relationships have changed since the Victorian era, and so have our internalized tensions.

The powerful father of Freud's time now appears to be in decline. The father, who, for Freud, symbolized the superego, often has less knowledge to impart to the child. Most children today, in fact, have little idea what their fathers actually do. The interaction of working life and family life so common in the past is now the exception, not the rule. Children are increasingly socialized by forces outside the family. No longer sheltered by the family, the child's ego cannot use the bonds of love to master interpersonal conflict. Instead, the child is subjected to the impersonal demands of institutions, such as schools, that discourage conflict and reward those who adapt. The bonds of love are replaced by the bonds of social approval.

Paternal authority is rapidly being replaced by technological authority. Like a father, the computer offers guidance, holding out the promise of a career and security. The individual even recognizes a kind of human quality in the computer that aids in this unprecedented shift in allegiance from man to machine: the computer's use of words, sounds, and commands are essentially representations of another human being communicating through the medium of a program.

100

Thus, the hidden wish to uproot the father is transformed. Aggression is now channeled toward trying to dominate the machine, to outperform it, "tearing apart" a program during debugging, for example. At times, aggression manifests itself as suppressed anger at co-workers who get in the way or are too slow, hindering one's productivity. From the point of view of work, adaptation is total.

This degree of adaptation sets the overspecialized character apart from all previous character types. The price of this overadaptation is a diminishing boundary between an individual's private psyche and the prevailing social psyche. People become more and more alike, standardized by the influence of social reality.

This is not a science fiction scenario. It is a trend that is already well underway. To counteract it, we need to take more enlightened approaches to the use of computer technology. We need to respect the human dimension in work and communication. And we need to reject the seductive notion that the values of the machine are values worthy of emulation.

# FIVE

## An End
## to Romance

"It's hard enough to get what you need from
a relationship—with a computer around it's
practically impossible."

*Jenny*
Computer widow

THE RECENT BIRTH of the new civilization in Silicon Valley heralds an end to romantic love as it has been known in Western civilization. Developed from the courtly ideal some seven centuries ago, romantic love has always offered a possibility for affirmation of one's self in union with another. As the nature and needs of the self are altered by electronic space, so is the nature of love.

There is no activity in life more important than forging and sustaining bonds with a romantic partner. Relationships are a constant concern for most of us. If we are unattached, the search for a romantic partner is often an obsession; our time, money, and thoughts are often devoted largely to that search. It takes us years to learn the elegant rituals of courtship—playing the suitor, learning the boundaries of appropriate behavior, knowing when intimacy is called for, and understanding unspoken clues revealing resentment, rejection, or hurt. Once a couple is formed, both partners must constantly relearn the subtleties of reciprocity and understanding—submerging our own immediate desires to our mate's, making decisions cooperatively, offering support and sharing confidences, developing enough trust to let down our defenses.

It is part of our nature to form couples. Divorced men and women, who sometimes vow they will never marry again, invariably return to the marriage market, and quickly. Try as we may, we cannot deny the importance of intimate attachments. Nevertheless, the bonds between people are easily broken. The energy we devote to making links with others is matched by the energy given off by the often stormy disintegration of relationships. Six and a half million Americans today are in psychotherapy, and a central topic in many sessions is the "meaningful relationship." A flood of self-help books written by psychologists has swamped bookstores in recent years. The marriage-counseling field, too, has seen a surge in the last decade. We have become a psychological society, and loneliness is our foremost preoccupation. When the computer enters our lives and begins to exert tugs and strains on our relationships, it is thus entering a tumultuous environment. As if there were not already enough obstacles in our path toward intimacy, the computer adds yet another.

103

Tolstoy began *Anna Karenina* with the observation, "Happy families are all alike; each unhappy family is unhappy in its own way." This has rung true to generations of readers, but the mass introduction of computers into the workplace has reversed it. Today, the families of technical workers are unhappy in the same way.

To be married to a technostress sufferer—male or female—is to experience emotional isolation.

Linda, an advertising executive, was married for seven years to Richard, a programmer who became director of computer services for a large bank. They had lived together for a year and a half before marrying, and during that time Linda found Richard to be a thoroughly warm and emotional person. He socialized regularly with a group of eight or nine friends. As Richard's computer skills increased, so did his salary, wardrobe, and hours, while his communication with Linda and friendships with others declined. Conversation became shop talk. Richard developed a protective shell, a stance that seemed to say, "I don't need people. I have nothing to talk about anymore."

At her job as a bank computer manager, Joann would typically isolate herself when she came home from work:

"Bad day?" her husband would ask.

"Yup."

"You want to talk about it?"

"Nope," she would say, and go into the bedroom and shut the door. Home existed for her as a place to recover from work, a place in which to pull herself together in order to face work again. She had no time for anything except survival. The only topic of conversation at home was her work. The mention of anything else, such as family matters or events in the news, led to fights.

Says Joann now: "The person who walked in that door after surviving ten hours with a dumb computer was not a nice person."

104

Richard is the classic technocentered worker. So was Joann, until she quit. People like these risk losing the capacity for genuine communication. Expressions of interest and emotion, of playfulness and spontaneity, of empathy for others, are restricted to a startling degree. Because of this, the technocentered individual is cut off from the world. This withdrawal can be painful for family and friends. In a world where relationships with others are such a crucial ingredient of happiness, loneliness can be devastating. Technocentered people do not themselves notice that they have isolated themselves, and in any case they consider their work to be a more appropriate subject of concern than such "soft" issues as relationships. The spouses and lovers of technocentered people must bear the brunt of the pain of isolation. As they watch, their life partners drift out of reach, leaving a void that for some is as hard to bear as if the spouse had disappeared.

Richard could relate to "Wash the car" and "Do the dishes," Linda recalls, but "How do you feel about that?" would bring forth a retort like, "What do you want from me?" Linda began studying the newspaper, just to be able to say something she thought Richard would listen to at dinner. "But he wasn't conversing," Linda says. "It was fact, fact—he was *fact*ing! Our entire conversation consisted of data. We exchanged random bits of unconnected information."

Technocentered people seem not so much isolated as

utterly alien. They lack a certain physical presence, an ability to gesture or use body language smoothly and gracefully; the image of the "computer nerd" comes readily to mind. Viewed as mere eccentricity, the out-of-sync quality of the total computer worker can have a comic aspect. A 1983 issue of *Psychology Today* contained a profile of Stanford University's John McCarthy, a pioneer in the field of artificial intelligence, a term that he himself coined in 1956.

> While most people can be said to socialize by talking to one another, McCarthy's manner of socializing at the laboratory consists mainly of walking around in the halls, stepping into an office here or there, picking up something from the desk, and reading it. "Sometimes he'll walk in when you're there, not say anything to you, just pick something up and read it, then walk out," [a colleague says]. . . . One researcher at Stanford recalls standing in the laboratory's snack room chatting with McCarthy about some problem. The researcher ended a sentence and turned to hear McCarthy's response. But McCarthy had disappeared. Two days later, the researcher was standing near the same spot. McCarthy walked up without greeting, and resumed the conversation midthought.

Whether Dr. McCarthy can be described as technocentered is not, of course, a matter that can be determined by reading a magazine profile. But he shares with the technocentered individual a tendency to relate to others entirely in terms of information exchange, an obliviousness to others, and a loss of social norms.

For a spouse or lover, the dwindling of communication can be disastrous. Technocentered people are reluctant to spend time talking about marital concerns or other matters that require emotional exchange or empathic attention to the other person's feelings. With the computer as their model, they view communication as data transfer. Intimate time disappears.

Bob is a research biochemist for a major drug company. He uses a computer to generate possible molecular configurations for new chemical compounds. Recently, he bought a computer so he could run experiments at home. He spends his evenings now watching the screen, hoping for new discoveries. On weekends, during the halftimes of televised football games, he runs to his den to observe the machine working.

Bob's conversations with his wife Nancy are brief and pointed. His thoughts are always elsewhere—usually directed toward what's happening on one screen or the other. "It's worse than being a Monday Night Football widow," Nancy says. When she tries to assert herself, Bob becomes angry. When she's quiet, he ignores her. She has contemplated unplugging the machine while he's working on it, but fears that this will ruin his experiment—and their relationship.

For the technocentered person, communication is strictly utilitarian. Brevity is essential, with yes-no answers always preferable ("Would you like to go out tonight, and if so, where?"). When conversation drifts into open-ended questions, the technocentered person becomes impatient. There is no room for ambiguity or nuance. Technocentered people insist on efficiency and rules: don't theorize, don't talk too much, don't digress, don't be obscure. Rules are, after all, the *sine qua non* of computers. Computers were invented to handle any job composed of "effective procedures," tasks that can be formalized according to rules written in precise and unambiguous language. Artificial intelligence researchers dream of formalizing rules of behavior and thought so that they can be incorporated in mind-mimicking computer programs. Technocentered people unwittingly invert this goal, striving to mirror the logic of the computer program in their own minds; their thoughts begin to resemble a series of effective procedures.

But most human activities defy precise rules. Our behavior is by nature ambiguous, beginning with the act of speaking to one another. Humans communicate using multiple channels—not only language but intonation, eye contact, gesture, facial expression, and so on. Language itself is imprecise. Many words have shades of meaning that become clear only in context, and sometimes not then. Diction can set the tone of an exchange: the same words can evoke charm or disdain, enthusiasm or anxiety. Social competence of the most ordinary kind demands an understanding of these subtleties. Without it, relationships remain perfunctory and intimacy impossible.

Alice has been married for eighteen years to Ron, a computer programmer for the last fifteen of those years. Ron handles the payroll system for the public works department of a large city. Alice has learned to live with the cancellation of vacations, phone calls in the middle of the night, "that kind of stuff—a lot of pressure." More difficult for Alice to endure, however, is Ron's completely analytical outlook on life. "If you need to pour out your problems," she says, "he's the kind of guy who sits there and coldly gets right down to the facts of the problem and what the solution should be. But a lot of times you don't want a solution. You just need someone to say that it's going to be okay, you'll be all right."

An outgrowth of technocentered individuals' disdain for ambiguity is a demand for order in their surroundings. Many technocentered people become disgruntled, for example, when cooking utensils or a favorite coffee cup are not in their usual place. Things misplaced are a violation of the rules and hence break the routine (or subroutine). Order and predictability become an obsession.

Sarah and Joseph have been married for five years. He is the manager of a data processing department. Sarah describes what she found suffocating about Joseph's world:

> Everywhere you looked, it was rationale to the left, logic to the right, scheduling right up ahead. Everything was structured. I remember a vacation we took.

There was no spontaneity allowed. If we left for the beach, he'd have to know beforehand what time we were going to get back to the hotel room. If I wanted to stop to see an interesting sight we passed on the road, he would refuse. "It's not on our agenda," he'd say.

Technocentered people become unable to switch contexts, to distinguish between home and office, or spouse and coworker. Normally, we shift contexts smoothly and unconsciously many times a day. We know we shouldn't calculate budget projections at the breakfast table, hum during staff meetings, or wear portable earphones in church. With the boss we make polite and deferential small talk, appear sincerely interested in all subjects discussed, and avoid belittling comments. With friends after work, on the other hand, we tease or interrupt one another, and ask personal questions. If we were to confuse these two contexts, we might end up losing both our friends and our job. Most of us have no trouble with this, however; we step from one situation into another and immediately alter our behavior to fit the surroundings. Shifting contexts is a skill that we take for granted, but one that we need in order to interact with others. For technocentered people, it is nearly impossible. They spout information when intimate conversation is appropriate. Spouses feel as though they are being "talked at" or having ideas "bounced off" them. Instead of a genuine dialogue with a complexity of messages, there is a monologue from each side.

The inability to shift contexts is one of the ways in which the technocentered person differs most noticeably from the obsessive-compulsive. Obsessives, always acting out a role, shift easily from work-mode to home-mode, from thinking "Now I am a doctor" to thinking "Now I am a husband/wife." For technocentered people, however, work determines the self. Home becomes not a place to assume a new role but a place in which either to shut down or, frequently, to continue working.

108

When not at his payroll-manager job, Alice's husband Ron sits in front of the television. "He has given up all his hobbies," says Alice. "He can't relax. He'll wake up in the middle of the night, and the answer to a problem will hit him. He'll have been dreaming about it. And in the evening, he'll sit there falling asleep in his chair and still talk to you about his work."

At least Ron is trying to communicate. In many relationships, communication stops completely; computer-think becomes an insurmountable barrier. This is particularly true when a computer is physically present in the home, in which case the technocentered person does not even make an effort to switch contexts. Work continues unabated.

Jennifer is among a growing number of women who are home-computer widows. Frank, her husband of twelve years, carts the personal computer he bought for his small business back and forth between his office and home, spending an average of three hours a day on it at the office and eight to ten hours a week at home. He is as excited about his home computer now as he was a year ago when he bought it, and finds a new use for it every other week or so.

Once Frank refused to finish up and move the machine from the dining room table when Jennifer was expecting some friends for lunch. He waited until her friends were actually in the door before moving it, and Jennifer was furious. "I remember the printer was hooked up to it," Jennifer says. "My hand was that far from grabbing all the wires and breaking the thing."

Much of the communication breakdown in these situations stems from the computer user's inability to take the "role of the other." This, as psychologist Carl Rogers has noted, is one of the most important factors in sustaining human relationships. It means, essentially, that one can empathize with another person and identify with what the other person perceives or feels.

Technocentered people are unable to feel the complex

emotions that empathy requires, and their spouses end up feeling rejected. Jennifer's husband Frank still tries to pay attention to her needs—he hasn't become completely technocentered—"but there's a feeling that I'm secondary in his life now," Jennifer says. "I don't really know when I have him and when I don't."

Jeremy describes life with Carol before she quit her programming job. "If I got her to leave the computer and come sit with me and watch TV or just read the paper together, in her mind she was still on the computer. All of a sudden she'd say, 'I've got it! If I just take the I/O board and . . .' Once in a dream Carol had, she actually became her Apple. She said she dreamed she went from I/O board to I/O board and visited the inside of the computer, and the next day she had a tremendous insight into the program she was working on, and that made her feel a whole lot closer to her Apple. I felt I was sharing her with the computer, barely. Most of the time I got nothing and the computer got everything."

Arnold, a manager of a corporate data-processing department, has been able to keep his work and home life separate. But when his wife, Kay, began taking an interest in computers and took a job as assistant to a systems analyst, Arnold suggested that they buy a personal computer so Kay could practice programming at home.

Arnold has recently noticed a change in his wife. She seems wrapped up in her computer activities, has little time for him, and grows impatient with him easily when they talk. Arnold finds the change hard to tolerate.

As an example of Kay's behavior, Arnold reports that one night in bed she turned to him and said, "Are you on-line tonight or not?" Arnold regrets encouraging Kay's computer use, feeling matters have gone too far. Kay is doing well at work, but their marriage is under strain.

It is interesting that although many women married to technocentered men feel unhappy with their situation, they rarely contemplate divorce or infidelity. Despite husbands who exhibited serious character defects, the wives accepted, on some level, their behavior as merely an exaggerated version of normalcy. After all, these men functioned well at work and were not hostile or abusive. When women were the technocentered partner, the husbands expressed greater anger and jealousy. Women, it would seem, are not supposed to take their careers—whatever they might be—as seriously as men do. Moreover, since women are expected to be more emotional, sensitive, and solicitous of their husbands' needs, the technocentered wife appears to be a greater aberration. But because the technocentered condition reaches so deeply into our psyche, it recognizes no sex-role difference.

111

Outside of marriage, the social relations of computer-obsessed individuals can best be described as "pseudo-attachments." For unattached technocentered workers, forming relationships of any kind is difficult; forming committed, long-term relationships is impossible. Asked about their stagnant social lives, they will say it's a matter of choice, or "it's not the right time in my life."

Jay came west after graduating from college three years ago to take his first job, as a computer programmer. His fiancée accompanied him, but nine months later they broke up. "She just had too many expectations of me. I didn't have time for romance anymore. It was time to grow up, and I couldn't spend all that time 'relating' and everything like we did in college." Today, Jay's relationships with women, who are themselves computer workers, are "efficient," and he seems to view the women themselves as interchangeable.

Technocentered workers, for whom control and predictability are all-important, have little room in their world for the uncontrollable, unpredictable power of lust. Lust in a broader sense—the drive to satisfy underlying human needs—is dampened, because the technocentered victims can't feel what their needs really are or whether they even have any. The concept is too abstract, and lust too illogical. Lust is superseded by the planning and control functions of the brain. Janet, a systems analyst, used to "plan" to have sex with her husband several days in advance. This way, she says, it would "fit into her schedule" and not disrupt her work-related activities. She had no feeling for herself as a sexual being directed by desire for her husband. Sex itself was a release of tension, not a positive drive.

Sexuality in this case is not so much repressed as controlled; it is incorporated into the new life-structure. The real source of immediacy, excitement, and power for the technocentered person is technical mastery. With it, one imagines rising above the needs and vulnerabilities of mere mortals and achieving what can only be described as omnipotence. This sense of omnipotence is a central characteristic of the technocentered person.

Ironically, while intense computer involvement can hamper lust for one's spouse or lover, it seems to stimulate lust in other ways. A popular form of computer use is networking, where users log onto computer-mediated conference calls with strangers identified only by their "handles." Participants commonly describe how they feel their inhibitions dropping away as they discourse intimately with strangers. Lindsay Van Gelder, a contributing editor to *Ms.* magazine, writes of plugging into a branch of the CompuServe computer network where users can pair off privately and send each other electronic messages like "I'm French-kissing you now." She describes this emerging form of erotica:

> One man who does it often (sometimes one-on-one, sometimes with his girlfriend in the room in an on-line orgy with another couple) described it as "like having a dirty book that talks back to you." Another man pointed out that you can't get AIDS or herpes from a keyboard. A woman told me that she even passes on the names of men who are "good CompuSex lovers." (No, I didn't try it—somehow, it seemed to qualify as genuine infidelity.)

As that last statement suggests, one can no longer easily separate what is lust from what is not when computers are the primary link with other people. When does data transfer become a relationship?

On the Source, a rival service to CompuServe, these metarelationships also flourish. One of the Source's in-house celebrities is Dave Hughes, a former Defense Department advisor who has stored his writings about the efficiency and intimacy of electronic relationships in CompuServe's central computer, where users can access them. Steve Levy, in a *Technology Illustrated* magazine article tells of a fully documented "electronic romance" between Hughes and a former Carter White House official, Ann Blocker:

> In her "Sorsex" Magazine [accessible via CompuServe] she describes how she accessed Dave's file: "Thirty minutes later, I was in love," she confided to 23,000 users, and then embarked on an extended ode to Sourcevoid Dave's visions. Dave, in turn, used Sourcetrek to describe his feelings about Ann, culminating in an epic poem, "A.Bouquet.of.Ions." (Sample: "So bite the Apple my sweet/That I may caress your nubile imagination/With these fingertips from afar.")

Whether the energy poured into such computer usage is an antisocial substitute for real-life relationships or a stimulating addition to them is impossible to say. There is evidence, however, that for many computer users the former is true. Gregg Easterbrook, writing in *The Washington Monthly*, points out that it is no longer just the math nerd in search of a calculus solution who is transfixed by the computer: people of all kinds are drawn to it because they feel less alone. People crave understanding and companionship, Easterbrook writes, and these are what computers give the appearance of providing, especially as voice activation and larger computer memories become feasible:

113

Consider, for instance, that perhaps 90 percent of the regular communication between people—even two close people, like husband and wife—is mundane. The bulk of daily conversation consists of simple, flat statements like, "what do you want," "wait a second," "I'm over here," and "it's pretty good." Moments of lyrical expression, or deep emotional contact, are rare even in the most intimate love affairs. . . . All of which is to say, most of what passes between human beings could easily be programmed into a computer. . . .

114

If this sounds like a Big Brother nightmare, think about it from the lonely person's perspective. Ours is a society where increasingly thousands—if not millions—of people live alone, fearing their neighbors, and with no social ties to family or church. . . . In this environment a talking computer, with some rudimentary awareness of its user's personal condition, which *always pays attention*, could be a blessing. It couldn't possibly provide true companionship, or the emotional heights experienced by lovers, friends, parents, and offspring. But it could keep that mundane chatter—the background noise of human relations—going at all times, providing an illusion of companionship.

Computer manufacturers and vendors have fostered this illusion by giving personal computers personal names like Lisa, Victor, and Adam and selling them as though they were selling some kind of mechanical pet. The key seems to be to present the technology as warm and inviting. The upshot is confusion—we are being asked to buy and use machines that are not *really* machines at all; they're too *friendly* to be machines. Some cultural commentators have used cozy images, like the "electronic cottage," to mask the mechanical realities of the computer, thus obscuring our ability to recognize the way technology can affect us. In *The Intimate Machine*, Neil Frude, who labels the new technology "soft" and the computer a "microcompanion," suggests:

The lonely, the isolated, and the disabled could benefit
even more than other people from advanced soft technology. The companion machine could provide much-
needed contact and companionship and would enable
lonely people to fill their lives with interest, conversation, and concern. . . . A socially skilled system could
introduce . . . two [lonely people], helping to start the
conversation and then retiring gracefully when the
human interaction has begun to flow. Companion machines would help people to be better informed and
offer a useful model for conversational skills; they
would also provide an interesting focus for talk, just
as dogs now often evoke comment and casual contact
between people in public places.

In fact, we know that the computer not only does not
possess the capacity to "retire gracefully," but once it has
become an integral part of human interaction, it alters the
content as well as the form of that interaction.

Marshall McLuhan once observed that modern communication technologies were turning the world into a
"global village" whose citizens could share and interact
intimately despite geographic distance. Margaret Mead,
however, accurately observed that in a real village the
inhabitants are close together; they watch each other,
touch each other, and share a common history. Electronic
communications, in her view, were no substitute for the
real thing.

The dynamics of the way machine-dependence actually interferes with face-to-face interaction remain to be
explored, but the problem may begin with that central
symptom of technostress: distortion of the user's sense of
time. Once the computer alters the user's sense of time,
social dysfunctions ensue. Those who live with computer
workers invariably complain that disputes over time are a
major source of friction. Jennifer, the home-computer
widow, says that if Frank has promised to take her somewhere at a specific time, she may as well cancel the
appointment if he begins to work at the computer. "He'll

plead, 'If you'll only give me five more minutes, I can get this done,' and three hours later he'll say, 'Gee, it's not doing what I want it to do. Just give me five more minutes.' " When she confronts him, Jennifer says he is "almost childlike" in putting her off: " 'While you're here, look at this! I want to show you the greatest thing I learned the other day—Look what it can do for us.' "

Memories of the past and hopes for the future are intangible yet vital parts of what makes a normal person tick. If we are half-computer, memory and hope diminish. Empathetic time, in which we allow ourselves to experience life in full, disappears. It is replaced by emptiness. Staring blankly, watching television, picturing ourselves making endless loops on an I/O board—all are autohypnotic activities, a way of filling time in a void.

The lonely spouse can react in many ways to situations such as these: resignation, fury, abandonment. Linda, tired of "facting," finally left Richard. "The only way I could have made the marriage work," she says, "is to have become floppy. You know, passive, totally floppy." Jennifer and Frank reached a compromise, with Frank promising to pay more attention to Jennifer's conversational needs. But the computer, says Jennifer, is still a problem for them:

> We've had to negotiate and renegotiate. The other negotiations that we have worked out in our marriage we both abide by, but this has been the most difficult one. We have always taken turns with household jobs so no one gets stuck doing the dishes all the time. I'll sit here thinking, all this stuff has to be done and he's just playing with the computer. He'll wait till the last minute, and then he'll be up washing dishes at one in the morning, but he gets it done.

When computer dependence is more advanced, negotiations are out of the question. The rejected spouse often goes to extremes to break through to the technocen-

116

tered partner. Jeremy, jealous of Carol's devotion to her computer, says that more than once he has smashed his wife's computer in what he calls "wild and crazy fits." Money is not a problem for the couple—Jeremy is president of his own Silicon Valley software company—and the next day Carol would buy another one, a luxury not yet available to the masses. "After you break the computer," Jeremy says, "you're going to feel bad, but having to experience her as half-computer . . . is just as bad." Although he also dealt with computers, it was as a businessman; he prided himself on selling programs, not creating or using them. 117

When a spouse turns violent or finally threatens to leave, technocentered people are forced for the first time to evaluate themselves and their actions by something other than a "performance mode." A choice is being forced on them: to change or face abandonment. Some opt for the latter. Others end up in a psychotherapist's office, where they resemble an active computer system whose plug has been pulled. When Jeremy and Carol went to a counseling session, the psychologist fared no better than her husband. "I can't talk about this—I feel like my head is going to implode," Carol told the therapist. "I have an inability to process data on this level."

Reorganization begins at this point. Sometimes, the victims decide to leave computer work for unrelated pursuits—gardening, taxi driving, carpentry, anything with less mental involvement—and the cycle of machine dependence is broken. Unlike the obsessive-compulsive, who remains driven in any milieu, the technocentered individual seems a new person in a new environment, capable of empathy and affection. "The day I gave notice," says Joann,

> I felt a tremendous sense of release. My life started to change immediately. I began to enjoy life. I enjoyed my home. I developed a real relationship with my husband. We decided we had a marriage after all. And

I started to grow as a person. The entire nine years
I managed that department, I wasn't developing. It's
strange to begin to grow at thirty.

"Since quitting her job, Carol's changing," says her
husband, Jeremy. "I find a new Carol now—more loving,
more sensuous, more of a human being. Before she quit,
I was only getting about two percent of the human part
of her."

Much psychological growth—and this remains true
from the moment we emerge from the womb until we
die—occurs, directly or indirectly, through interaction
with other humans. We so often hear people say they "just
can't make a commitment" to a personal relationship.
Commitment is often difficult for us, accustomed as we are
to changing jobs, houses, friends. A commitment to
another is built on dialogue and an understanding of one's
own needs as well as the other's. To truly commit ourselves, we must move beyond our fears that we may lose
the object of our commitment. Often, we find it easier to
make commitments to our jobs than to other people; people
are unpredictable, harder to trust, and full of inconsisten-
cies. Yet despite the obstacles to intimacy, psychologically
healthy individuals continue to struggle to reach out and
make commitments to others.

The opportunity for growth is never greater than
within the psychologically intimate relationship that is possible between parent and child, or within an intimate,
erotic relationship between two adults. This was not always so: traditionally, marriage and adulthood were both
regarded as static states. Today, our expectations of marriage are changing. We recognize that people continue to
develop throughout their lives, and that these patterns of
growth are a necessary and positive part of the life cycle.
An intimate relationship provides the emotional security
that allows people the freedom to make choices, cope with
problems, and meet challenges.

As the nature and needs of the self are distorted by

identification with the computer, so is the nature of intimacy. When the mind of one's mate is a logic loop and intimacy becomes impossible, one's own growth suffers.

When our growth is threatened, so is our humanity. As human beings, we have a limitless potential for experiencing feelings and sharing them with others, a potential far beyond that of other species. Direct and intimate communication is important to many social relationships, not only romantic ones. Intimacy is one of the hallmarks of any close friendship. Psychologist Sidney Jourard, in his book *The Transparent Self,* focused on this aspect of social relationships in terms of what he called self-disclosure. For Jourard, self-disclosure meant that a person "discloses his experience to another, fully, spontaneously, and honestly." Jourard observed a correlation between self-disclosure and psychological well-being:

> When a man does not acknowledge to himself who, what, and how he is, he is out of touch with reality, and he will sicken. No one can help him without access to the facts. And it seems to be another fact that no man can come to know himself except as an outcome of disclosure to another person.

Under the spell of the machine, we are at risk of losing that special ability of humans to be intimate. Noticing, understanding, and communicating our feelings is a skill as much as a tendency. As a skill, it requires time, practice, learning, and nurturing. If we disregard our potential for articulating our feelings, that potential can wither—and so can our humanness.

Modern love is, in a sense, newly fashionable. In years past, marriages were arranged, and love, lust, and emotions were not a factor. We could easily revert to those times. Our concept of normalcy shifts from generation to generation. Homosexuality, for example, is no longer considered a mental illness, whereas machismo has just been designated a neurosis by the American Psychiatric Association. Who is to say that the robot/human—human/robot of 1984 will not be the spouse of choice in 2034? Technocentered individuals, when diagnosed, may not always be dismissed as aberrations, for they may be seen as harbingers of the future.

If this occurs, it will be a step backward for all of us. Even gorillas reveal their emotions to one another. They frown when annoyed, they bite their lips when undecided, and their young throw tantrums when thwarted. If we allow technocenteredness to thrive unchallenged and untreated, we may reach a point in evolution when groups of gorillas in the field will seem more human than the workers in modern cities do.

120

# SIX

## Childhood Lost

"Sometimes I feel lonely, but I'd rather be with the computer than with my friends."

*Bobby*
Age 10

A SUMMER 1983 headline in *USA Today*, the national tabloid coming to us "via satellite," read "USA's Whiz Kids Rule the Computer World," and the full-color cover story was subtitled, "They show their elders new ways to think." The story described startling accomplishments by youngsters: an eleven-year-old in Texas writes a syndicated newspaper column about computers; numerous children across the country make substantial sums of money (up to $60,000 a year) inventing computer games; a sixteen-year-old in California has founded a company that offers uncopiable systems to protect against computer piracy. His company is a leader in the field. One seventeen-year-old in New Jersey helped his school system buy seventy-six computers and trained teachers to operate them, and was then hired by a New York firm to rewrite the software. He is about to graduate from high school and, in the words of his principal, has "been recruited as if he were a seven-foot basketball player." The youngster spoke at his old elementary school, and, says one of those attending, "it was like Rocky. The kids were standing up and cheering."

The juvenile computer hotshot is the new culture hero. Apple Computer's cofounder, Steven Jobs, is still in his late twenties—"old" in the computer world, as Jobs himself admits. No longer are we surprised to read about teenage video-game designers or software tycoons too young to vote, and as personal computers flood the nation's homes and schools, our children are taking heed of these new role models.

And yet a closer look shows danger signs. Some of these role models are engaged in illegal pursuits; specialists at breaking into computer systems at will, they can dial up the school computer to alter grades, order free cases of soda by diverting delivery trucks, or make free phone calls all over the world. Kids who are thrilled playing video games absorb the violent content of those games: Space Invaders, Asteroids, Defender, and Galaxian all involve one form of annihilation or another. And there is another, more insidious danger: as with adults, heavy computer use threatens to distort a child's ability to learn and to interact with others as a healthy human being. The frightening fact is that adults are encouraging rather than combating this trend.

We are approaching a new era in which adults will learn from the intelligent young. This turn of events was foreseen by anthropologist Margaret Mead not long before her death. Throughout her career, Mead examined the changes in the way culture is transmitted from one generation to the next, especially from parent to child. In *Culture and Commitment* she wrote of three cultural styles: the postfigurative, or traditional; the cofigurative, that in which most of us have grown up; and the prefigurative, which, as she foresaw, is now upon us.

A postfigurative culture is one in which change is so imperceptibly slow "that grandparents, holding newborn grandchildren in their arms, cannot conceive of any other future for the children than their own past lives." The past of the adult is the future of the child. There is an unquestioned sense of the rightness of each known aspect of life, however painful or difficult the various passages may be.

A cofigurative culture is one in which old and young alike assume that it is natural for the behavior of each new generation to differ from that of the preceding generation, although elders still dominate by placing limits on the young. A shift to cofiguration can come about for a number of reasons: after a migration leaves the elders in the positions of immigrants and strangers, after a war in which the defeated population must learn a new language and way of life, or after new technologies are introduced in which the elders are unskilled. The young now differ from their ancestors. Conflicts between generations become commonplace, and childhood itself becomes precarious. The young create and discard new values, and the ties of a youth culture usurp the strength of family bonds. Flexibility becomes important: young people must not only learn new skills but find personal meaning and justification in what they do. The cofigurative society is familiar to most of us: we are different from our parents and our grandparents. Our lives are characterized by change, by struggles over values and styles of living.

124

In a prefigurative culture, an accelerated rate of change, pushed forward by rapid changes in technology, is the norm. Values and styles of living change within a generation. The thinking of adults not only ill prepares their children for the world they will face, but limits them. Children are abandoned to the immediacy of experience in a world no one understands, but one in which the children's freedom from the past is an advantage.

Today's technological society is prefigurative. Having moved into a present for which the past has not prepared us, we increasingly encounter the articulate young who ask questions we have never thought to ask and who have mastered tools with which we have not worked. Mead found in the past no parallel to this contemporary form of culture. She pointed out that today everyone born before World War II is "an immigrant in time," ignorant of the meaning of the electronic revolution. Today, that assessment should probably be updated. As Charles Lecht, a New York computer executive, told *Time* magazine, "If you were born before 1965 . . . you're going to be out of it."

A reversal of relationships between generations has been set in motion. Adults look to children for help in using computers. A computer teacher at the University of Kansas described a typical example: an adult student brought her son to class for the first few weeks so that she could watch him do the class assignments first. Herbert Kohl, an educator writing in *Harvard Magazine,* described the phenomenon of children as young as nine using computer stores as a social center: "As long as they made no trouble and freed the machines for customers, they were welcome. In fact, they were very helpful to the salespeople, because some of them knew more about computers and computing than anyone who worked at the store." Many adults find this role reversal unsettling. "Did you ever play Pac-Man in front of a crowd of thirteen-year-old sharks whispering to each other about 'P-4 tunnel patterns' and barely suppressing snickers?" asks *Personal Computing*'s David Grady. In the home, this state of affairs can become a more serious source of anxiety or irritation. Many a father has plugged in the new home computer only to feel the discomforting gaze of his elementary-aged children watching impatiently—and expertly—over his shoulder.

125

Mead opined that in order to bridge this new generation gap, "a degree of trust must be reestablished so that elders will be permitted to work with the young on the answers" to the new generation of questions. She believed this new working relationship would characterize the new era. Mead's general descriptive observations are solid, but her analysis of the dawning prefigurative culture is faulty. She missed the complexity of the emerging electronic culture, and her simple and hopeful view of it is strikingly inadequate.

Children today are weathering the same cultural forces as electronic office workers. Despite the self-congratulatory tone of most computers-and-kids stories in newspapers and magazines and PTA bulletins, techno-stress is becoming a factor in even young children. Many computer-involved youngsters suffer from the same mental strain, alteration of time, tyranny of perfection, mechanical social relations, and isolation that technostressed adults experience.

Our sense of time is altered by many processes in our lives. We are born rhythmic; our hearts beat, we breathe, our bodies move in coordinated patterns. We learn to match the inner rhythms of our lives with the outer rhythms of our environment and its schedules. Our sense of time develops as we do. The Swiss psychologist Jean Piaget discovered that children learn to understand time, like all logical thought, in stages. The child first learns to distinguish what comes before from what comes after, and then learns to notice durations.

For the computer-involved child, the notion of time is altered by computer use. First, the objective measurement of duration is temporarily lost. Time seems to elapse in a dream with no boundaries and no border. Here are some responses from computer-involved children when asked to give examples of losing track of time:

*Mark (age 12):* One time I figured out how to do graphics. There are thick lines and thin lines, and I was just playing with it. I spent four or five hours just doing it, and this was on a Sunday. I thought it was only one or two; I didn't know what had happened. Because it's really really weird—you're working away and then Mom calls, "Dinner!" Dinner? We just had lunch. And it's confusing for me. It's like falling asleep and thinking you've only been asleep fifteen minutes but you've actually been sleeping the whole night. You try to figure out where the time went. It went into the computer.

*Daniel (age 16):* Okay, every programmer gets bugs. That's considered normal. And if you can accept that, things may go along okay, and so you may get absorbed, keep programming for a long time, without knowing. Sometimes I stay after school. And suddenly I look up or remember that I should be home already. Hours pass like minutes.

You might have gotten a lot done. It's not that you're just dead lost and staring there like a zombie. You're doing something. All your ties are with the computer and none with the outside world. There's a little clock on the screen, so I don't miss classes when I work at school, but sometimes even that happens, particularly when it's real quiet.

Some regard this total involvement with the computer as evidence of the child's "addiction." While they are right in being alert to a potential danger, the nature of the problem is not a psychological addiction at all but a time warp. The child has realigned his or her measurement of time.

> *Mark:* You don't come home and say, "Okay, I've *got* to work on the computer." Like, if you're smoking, "I've *got* to have a cigarette. Where are the cigarettes?" It's not like that. It's just, once you've started, it's hard to stop.

One explanation for the loss of time is that when we are deeply involved in any activity we lose track of time. Kids playing baseball after school often forget to come home for dinner, too. Piaget notes that the notion of time depends to a large extent on what it is we are doing:

> We are all well aware that an interesting task seems to cover a shorter period of time than a boring one. What is interesting . . . is a mobilization of the strength of the individual when he wholeheartedly attacks a task important to him. On the other hand, boredom, disinterest, dissociation can cause visible diminution of strength, in other words a shutting off of available energy.

The difference in the ways children lose themselves playing baseball and using computers, however, is striking. Baseball, like other typical children's pursuits, is stimulating in a variety of ways. Baseball players are interacting with each other, learning about teamwork and competition, enjoying exercise, chatter, and camaraderie, honing eye-hand coordination and peripheral vision, coping with quiet spells and pressure situations, learning to accept defeat and victory gracefully. It is, in sum, a social activity. Computer work, by contrast, is usually a solitary, antisocial pursuit, generally devoid of demands on the imagination. Outside stimuli are shut off. Because parents think that refining computer skills is advantageous for their children, they often approve when their children are lost in the computer time warp; but they ignore the cost to the child.

128

Piaget was fascinated by the way children view time, and he devised an experiment to study the question. He would show a child two sequences of pictures in rapid succession, first sixteen pictures in four seconds and then thirty-two pictures in four seconds. He found that children younger than eight years old tended to think the second, more rapid sequence took longer. Children eight and older generally perceived the reverse: more events within a time span seemed to take less time.

The essence of the computer is speed. Because events occur with great frequency, their duration appears shorter. There is only a stream of mental events, without the dilution of motor activity. The child must constantly make decisions, choose directions, react to outputs on the screen. The computer user cannot stray too far from the prescribed logic of orderly, well-structured procedures, or the computer will not respond. The speed and intensity of this activity heightens the sense of engagement the child experiences with the work. In general, there is a reduction of external sensory experience. The outside world fades, and the child becomes locked into the machine's world.

Children cannot reduce their sensory inputs without closing off their interactions with others, and, as with adult computer workers, time distortion and social isolation go hand in hand. Parents may notice that a problem exists when a child has difficulty shifting contexts, from computer to people, or from computer to homework. The computer involvement begins to color all other interactions. In extreme cases, children develop an intolerance for human relationships. They become accustomed to high-frequency logic, a rapid-fire dialogue between screen and fingertips that makes time seem to speed up. In talking with parents, siblings, even friends, time drags by comparison. The only way to make the transition from machine to human is to talk about computers.

> *Ian (age 13):* I feel teachers talk too much. They could say half as much and be more efficient. The one I had last year just liked to lecture and never got to the point. In regular conversations you're just doing something to use up time. You don't do it unless you've got time to waste.
>
> *James (age 16):* Sometimes it's hard to switch over [from programming to family activities]. Work with the computer is like being in a bubble. Once my bubble's broken all the liquid flops out, and then I can be outside again. I shake once or twice, and I'm back in the real world again, trying to function like normal.
>
> *Matt (age 16):* Everything I say isn't . . . computer this and computer that. . . . but a lot of it is because my friends know what I'm talking about. . . . This gives me satisfaction. I don't have to talk things out a lot. It's like writing things out longhand—I don't like doing that either. I like to do things faster and better.

For young, intensely involved computer users, this altered sense of time is also changing their attitudes toward traditional learning media, such as books.

> *Tom (age 13):* You know, a computer is more like real life. Real life is something that's actually happening. In a way, books are real life because you're thinking about them happening while you're reading, but in a

computer, you're actually there doing it instead of reading about something that's happening. You're there in a computer. You're part of what's happening, and it's faster . . .

In making the shift from the computer to other contexts, one is forced to come to grips with the intangibles of the world—subtlety, reflection, sensory awareness, imagination. Children perceive this requirement as slowing them down. When a child is interacting with a computer, everything "clicks." Barriers between the child and the activity are at a minimum. The computer seems to pull the child right in.

In *On the Experience of Time*, Robert Ornstein notes that we normally use coding schemes to save energy when we digest information from the world. For example, if we hear the sequence of numbers 149217761945 read to us and are asked to remember them, we will have difficulty— unless we are told they are the dates Columbus discovered America, the Declaration of Independence was signed, and World War II ended. It is easier to remember three chunks (and familiar ones) than twelve random ones. Coding tricks like "chunking" apply to higher-level information and events as well. Human communication is complex. The codes to understand it are not always clear to adults, and they are less so to children. Human communication is difficult to "chunk"—it is inefficient, subject to interpretation, and hard to categorize. Since children don't have the experience or background to use human coding, they adapt more quickly to the sparse and uncomplicated coding of the computer. In conversation with an adult who does not speak in short, clear bits, they are more apt to be frustrated.

The same is true of reading. Reflecting on a story, imagining what the characters are going through, and wondering about the story's meaning all require the brain to process a great deal of information, and this can make time seem to slow down. For some children, this is a disin-

centive. The outside world provides challenges that require creative energy and new resources; the computer
provides efficient communication. Kids being raised by machines prefer efficient communication.

For some children, computer use also changes inner
standards of perfection. This can be a source of unhappi-
ness for those who attempt to measure up to the computer's own standards of perfection and, of course, fail.

> *Alice (age 13):* I usually don't expect to write out a
> program and then not have any errors. But when I get
> an error, I get that fixed, and then I come to another
> error. And by the time I get about four errors, I'm
> questioning whether or not it's worth going on.
> Maybe the whole thing isn't worth it.

> *Robert (age 16):* I hate it [making an error]. You try
> and get around that kind of thing. It could destroy
> you. I bought an uncrasher for my computer, which
> will basically uncrash the computer if it's crashed—in
> other words, frozen, messed up. You can get out of it
> and get into a monitor where you can see what you've
> done. Sometimes when you make a mistake, it de-
> stroys what you've done. Sometimes I'd like to de-
> stroy it.

Children with high-level computer skills tend to be
most self-accepting when they can be as error-free as the
computer. They apply more critical standards to themselves than parents or teachers typically do. In extreme
cases, they seem to model themselves on the computer,
rather than on their parents. They seem rigid, impatient
with themselves, unwilling to risk a fall from grace. But
even as they express frustration with themselves, they
view the computer novice with condescension or disdain.
Adults are sometimes seen as not merely slow, but

stupid. John, age 12, was asked by his mother to teach her about the computer. He comments:

> Well, it's kind of neat to not be always taught and to be able to teach, in a way, and sometimes it can sort of drag you when you're talking about something, and Mom's going, "What's going on?" I don't think I make a very good teacher myself. I'm too impatient. In the computer one comes after two—it's just taken for granted one comes after two—whereas when you're teaching somebody sometimes they come up with questions like, "Why does one come after two?" Or two after one. It's frustrating. I just get sort of bored. I turn off and think, oh my God, who wants to do this? I'd rather get back to programming.

In general, John could not tolerate why-questions. They took time to answer, and the answers were always ones that "should" have been known.

When computer involvement is heavy, the distortion of time and drive for perfection while on the computer are unlike any experience young people have had before. In sports, one is limited by sore muscles or physical weariness. There are cues to tiredness in other activities such as practicing music, reading, or just playing "pretend" games. The attention span is naturally broken by stiff fingers, tired eyes, or a shift in imagination. Working with computers, the limit is mental exhaustion. Children, like adults, do not readily recognize the signs of mental fatigue. If they don't stop working, they experience a kind of depletion. Only by being alone can they recuperate.

> *Daniel (age 16):* After a day of programming, generally I'm pretty grumpy. I save what I have on disk, or if it's really going bad, I will just turn it off and get rid of the whole thing, the steps that frustrated me. And then I'm reasonably free of it. The biggest problem with relating to my family is they get demanding. They want me to talk with them, especially my

mother. But I don't want to do that. I'm tired. I'm edgy. I just want to be left alone.

*James (age 16):* After a hard day programming, I'm usually tired or upset. I try to go on to something that has nothing to do with computers. That's rough because I'm cranky and nothing else goes well. You know, it's like you were working on a big dinner and you accidentally left the stove on for an hour more than you were supposed to. . . . Mom and Dad see I get really upset and notice it when I don't want them around. They don't really say anything. I don't like people to console me or anything like that. So they don't do it anymore.

This compulsion to be alone after intense computer work is common among children. The mental fatigue they experience is similar to that of adult computer workers, and they realize it is different from other types of fatigue. They are undoubtedly the first generation of children to know such an experience.

In general, children do not become technocentered in quite the same way as adults, but they exhibit similar symptoms. The children at greatest risk are those who no longer notice that their computer work is causing them problems—shifting contexts from computer to conversation, for example, or missing meals. Once children begin to deny seeing anything wrong with their computer-centered behavior, there is cause for alarm. Some children claim to have no idea of the difference between using a computer and dealing with people. They may be flat in their self-expression, stiff and even a bit haggard in their appearance. Many betray an obvious, impatient sense of superiority, as if the technology has imbued them with power. In interviews, they may be impatient and report their experiences as if they were machines spewing out data, speaking volubly about minutiae having to do with computers but finding questions about feelings to be too vague to answer.

Children like these have the appearance of miniature

grownups. They seem to have command over their lives, but it is really only control over a technology. In their eerie resemblance to technocentered adults, they give us the first inkling that the computer is leveling the differences between the generations in an unhealthy way.

What is most alarming is that at formative stages in their lives, their basic personalities are being profoundly influenced by a machine—not a parent, teacher, coach, older sibling, or other human role model. A youth misspent at the terminal will influence development in later life. Adolescence is a crucial development stage, and teenagers from thirteen to seventeen, those "showing their elders new ways to think," are most at risk. As Eric Erikson has so eloquently pointed out, this age is a key time in the reorganization of personality from infancy, a time when we reorder our past life, a time when we establish our identity. Much of who we are as people, our attitudes and feelings about the world, are formed at this age. Adolescents are dealing with the stress of thinking about careers, about sexuality, and about social roles. Because of this, they are particularly vulnerable to technostress. The computer can become a refuge from the problems and conflicts of the real world, and well-rounded development and maturity can suffer.

Parents and teachers, for whom the computer is often a novelty and who are unfamiliar with the risks of intense computer involvement, usually admire their children's use of the technology. Often they actively encourage it, packing children off to summer computer camps and pushing for more school computers even while other school expenditures are being cut back. The current wisdom is that computer literacy is the newest and most important addition to the three Rs, a boost for children in their uncertain trek toward a happy future. Many assuage concerns about the merits of computer literacy by pointing out the children's own open-armed acceptance of computers, as though nothing could be more natural. They ignore or overlook the effects of unhealthy attachment to machines,

134

effects that can block the essential psychological processes of adolescence and lead instead to children who are less social, less flexible in their approach to learning, and less active physically as they become more computer dependent—in sum, personalities that are overspecialized at an early age.

Television was the last major technology that we invested in en masse. A scant thirty-five years ago, it held the promise of educating the young and bringing culture to the masses. Today, commercial television programming is viewed by many as a vast wasteland. Instead of educating the mind, it puts it on hold.

Television has served several purposes, however. It provides parents with an inexpensive babysitter, a chatty companion around the house, and an aid to relaxation after work. Some parents may object to their children watching it for hours on end every day, but most accept at least some TV-watching as a natural part of family life. In families where parents are often absent, television becomes a sort of surrogate parent.

To parents who are looking for a device to replace the mindlessness of television, the personal computer seems to be a boon. It appeals to their sense of what a parent should provide for a child: companionship, conversation, modernity. But more than this, it alleviates parents' fears that their children are wasting their leisure hours with some mindless diversion like TV. Parents reason that these machines help their children learn and ultimately get ahead at school. In fact, this replacement of the TV with a computer has created new problems.

Frances recently bought a home computer for her eleven-year-old son, Bill. "I thought I was doing something good when I bought the computer," she says. "I figured Bill would like it and watch TV less. The problem is now it's the thing he likes to do most. He always had difficulty playing with other kids, but now he doesn't even make an attempt. I'm sorry I ever brought it home." Despite her disapproval, Frances makes no effort to restrict Bill's access to the computer. Bill, for his part, says that his parents are usually not home and that he uses the computer for companionship. Asked why he doesn't play with other children, he says he isn't interested.

Jon, a single parent, bought his fifteen-year-old son, David, a computer so that David would stop demanding his attention during the evening. Jon figured that the computer would kill two birds with one stone: his son would develop computer skills and learn to keep himself occupied.

David has, in fact, done this. He spends little time with his father now, or with his younger brother. He finishes dinner, helps clear the table, and returns to the den where the computer is. While he works on his programs, his brother watches TV and his father takes care of work he brings home from the office. On some evenings there is a break to eat ice cream together.

Jon now confesses that his idea may have gotten out of hand. He complains of the lack of contact with his sons and says he misses the old routine hassles. David, at this point, prefers doing his programming and wants to be left alone. His father's interruptions irritate him.

Frances and Jon are typical examples of parents who introduce computers to their children as a way to solve their problems. Certain trends seem to be emerging quickly. First, many parents feel guilty about not spending more time with their children, especially in families where both parents work; to compensate for the lack of real attention, they buy computers for the children. The children, in turn, accept the computer because it is both a source of stimulation and a means of winning parental approval. Second, once the children grow attached to the computer, the parents are hesitant to break the bond because they can offer no substitute activity and because they believe the computer skills will benefit the children in the long run.

The least powerful member of the parent-child-computer triangle—the child—is at a disadvantage. The computer only reinforces the child's original problem: in David's case, it is the inability to get enough attention from his father; in Bill's case, it is a sense of loneliness around the house. Far from curbing a child's isolation, the computer increases it. Heavy involvement with the computer can encourage the child to put off dealing with the normal conflicts and personal problems of adolescence. In addition, when this triangle is created, communication between parent and child often becomes circumscribed. Questions about school or friends or other general conversation is reduced to questions about how work on the computer is going. After a while, the only relation between parent and child is a technical one. Unlike other common adolescent obsessions, the computer has a direct and powerful impact on the user's mental processes, and social and emotional isolation are reinforced.

137

Computer whiz kids earn recognition for their proficiency at the computer, for staying out of trouble, and for being productive. Adults view computer use as a form of work, and our culture still worships the work ethic. But when a child receives reinforcement only for performing, psychological problems in adult life inevitably ensue. In *Prisoners of Childhood,* psychologist Alice Miller notes that patients who were given praise and love primarily for performing activities well as children developed in adult life a depressing narcissism, capable of giving and receiving love only when they were productive. When they did not meet their own standards of perfection, they felt depressed.

Learning how to love takes time and openness, two qualities that the young computer whiz is unprepared to give. The computer may not prevent a child from expressing affection or other emotions, but an unhealthy dependence on it as a source of approval from adults reinforces any tendency a child might have toward antisocial behavior. It is the introverted child who is at greatest risk. Children with poorly developed social skills, for example, find it easier to cope with the awkwardness of adolescence if they spend their time on a computer. In moderation, this is perfectly natural, but in extreme cases the adolescent never has the chance to use the traumas of this difficult time to develop the new emotional perspectives necessary for psychological maturity.

A less acute problem is stress among the less adept computer users. Most children are not computer whizzes—to play with computer software is not the same as to lose oneself in programming—but teachers and parents are beginning to point to the class computer expert as a role model. The young computer expert is becoming the hero of the class, and every hero has worshippers. Teachers look kindly on kids who respond well to lessons. We must be careful that teachers and parents don't become enthralled with this brave new breed of heroes.

Ellen is a high school student. She is achievement-oriented and has an excellent grade point average. Last year, she took a class in learning to work with computers, but she couldn't seem to master it. She was often brought to tears by her experiences and envied thosed who succeeded. She began to complain of headaches and a nervous stomach at home. She become afraid that she would fall behind. Eventually, she learned to use the computer only to play games.

Too often, parents and teachers assume that a bright child will naturally become computer literate. This creates stress among children who are not interested in computers, *and there are many of them,* despite gleeful press reports to the contrary. The fact is that children do not take to computers automatically. Perhaps one child in three resists learning to use them, even for playing games. These tend to be girls, but not always. Most boys seem to be fascinated by computers, but the boy who doesn't understand them, cannot cope with them, or simply doesn't care comes under more pressure than does his female counterpart; he is less likely to confess what a girl will freely admit—that he is just not interested in computers.

138

For both boys and girls, to fail at computer literacy can be a humiliating experience.

We can only guess what effect technostress in parents has on their children. Certainly, if a parent is emotionally stunted, the child suffers. Harvard pediatrician T. Barry Brazelton has made some remarkable films of mother-infant interactions. He recorded the stimulation rhythms of healthy infants, the body movements and eye contact, the eager wiggle saying "pick me up" and the uncomfortable squirm saying "let me go." Both of these types of signals must be respected. Stimulation beyond the infant's ability to handle it is intrusive and makes it wary. Not enough stimulation makes the infant depressed. It is in fact by a subtle rhythmic process of drawing infants into human contact and then allowing them to withdraw that parents make babies into human beings. Brazelton captured on film the parental obliviousness that produces in the infant the syndrome known as "failure to thrive." A baby handled as an object becomes sluggish and inert and ceases to respond.

139

The absence of love is only part of the problem. The child also is deprived of a role model. Educational consultant John M. Morris, writing in *Educational Psychology*, referred to experiments where baby monkeys were raised without mothers but, instead, were given surrogate mothers constructed of rags and wire: "These surrogates provided the babies with all their needs, except one: the chance to observe what it was like to be an adult monkey. When the babies survived, they appeared to be seriously psychotic."

This model of human, responsive, ethical behavior is crucial to a child's development. It is a model that the technocentered parent is unable to provide. Obliviousness to a child's needs, the inability to read unspoken signals, is apparent in technocentered adults. In this way, the problems arising from machine-identification threaten to spread and worsen as today's children mature and new, mechanized norms of behavior are established and accepted.

Psychoanalyst Bruno Bettelheim has recorded the story of Joey, a schizophrenic child who functioned as if by remote control, plugging himself in and turning himself on before speaking. When the "machine" was not working, Bettelheim and his staff would find themselves forgetting that Joey was there, for he seemed not to exist. Bettelheim noted: "Again and again his acting-out of his delusions froze our own ability to respond as human beings." Joey's delusions, according to Bettelheim, are not uncommon among schizophrenic children today. They want to be rid of their unbearable humanity, to become completely automatic. Often their parents have treated them as objects from infancy. They are not cuddled or played with and were touched only when necessary.

Like many contemporary psychoanalysts, Bettelheim viewed schizophrenic patients as partly visionary: they can see and feel things that normal people cannot, and can often serve as weathervanes for changes in the culture that may eventually affect everyone. From this perspective, Joey's case can be regarded as prophetic.

# SEVEN

## Video Kids

"The children are as excited about learning how a caterpillar becomes a butterfly as they are about computers."

*Betsy*
First grade teacher

THE ENORMOUS INTEREST and affinity children have shown for video games has been a problem for many parents, who tend to feel games are a waste of time and, if the children are doing their game-playing in arcades rather than at home, a waste of money. Until 1982 and 1983 little serious research had been done to determine why video games are so attractive—and addictive—to children. However, two cognitive psychologists, Elizabeth and Jeff Loftus, provided three reasons in a book called *Mind at Play: The Psychology of Video Games.* First, players can improve their skills noticeably over a short period of time. Second, like a science fiction novel, a video game provides an alternate world in which to operate; mistakes can always be corrected, even if this calls for another quarter. Third, the games themselves adapt to the player: game speed, response time, and level of difficulty often change automatically according to how the player is faring. This contrasts with pinball, for instance, where the game design never changes. While the Loftuses use these characteristics to account for the children's addiction, which they define as "not being able to alter behavior willfully," they do not delve into the deeper implications of game playing: how does heavy video-game use affect a child's social and personal life? Is the current generation of children as a group different today as a result of video games? What difficulties are emerging?

With new technologies like home computers and video games, the concept of "generations of technology" is speeded up. Young children between seven and ten years old today can distinguish readily between the pre-video-game and post-video-game eras. Children in this age group who play at least an hour a day of video games for at least a year are substantially different from other children their age. As is true with adults and older children, time seems to accelerate for these young game-players. Patience is easily exhausted.

> *Maddy (age 7):* I can play five games on the Atari by the time it takes me to move one piece on the Monopoly board. Monopoly's so slow!

> *Lee (age 8):* Old games are different from video. You have to roll the dice, pick up cards, or hit a ball. In video, you're standing or sitting and you move your arms around. Everything goes fast!

At this age, it is important that children learn about controlling their impulses. They need to learn to "wait their turn" and suppress their desire for instant gratification. Video appeals to impulsive thinking, as though there were an electrical connection between the child and the game.

> *Megan (age 7):* I'm not used to regular games. They're hard to do. I can't concentrate on them. Video is faster. You don't have to bounce the ball.

> *Bobby (age 9):* It feels sad to play two-square. You want to be playing video. You're used to video. You think about it more than regular games. . . . You can't get hurt playing video games.

Given a choice between playing sports and video games, young children often prefer video games. In this alternative world, there is no physical danger. You can't get hit with a soccer ball, break your glasses, or fall off the gym bar. But the child who stops playing physical games begins to lose hand-eye coordination and other kinesthetic abilities. The child does less well at those occasional sports

143

attempted, and that in turn dampens interest even more. The fantasy world begins to gain an edge over the real world. When this happens, the social and developmental skills engendered by sports suffer as well. Instead, alone, often silent, unsmiling, and largely immobile, the child battles the machine.

Video games also change a child's perception of television. TV begins to seem more "boring" than ever before.

> *Alice (age 8):* I watched a lot of TV before. I enjoyed it. But now it bugs me. You can't plug the handle into the TV and control the men so that they fly up in the air. . . . Sometimes I take the paddles and turn on the TV and pretend I can move the people.

> *Jon (age 10):* TV is boring. You get tired of it quickly, it's so slow. There's nothing to do. Before [video], I didn't get so tired.

While parents may rejoice that their children are gaining a more critical view of television, the alteration of their children's sense of time is producing other important effects. The kids perceive instructions from adults in general and teachers in particular as bothersome. Their objection is not primarily a matter of testing authority or bridling at limits. In many cases, children feel that teachers are too slow in communicating instruction.

> *Alice (age 7):* The computer says "jump over," "turn," "turn right," "you fell down," or "you did it!" It doesn't use many words. . . . The teacher uses too many words. She teaches me too slowly.

> *Don (age 9):* Atari cartridges are neat! They come on and tell you what to do. They make it simple. Teachers talk slower than Atari, sometimes they make me angry. I think, "Come on, I want to go back to Atari. It tells me things faster than you do."

Many teachers report difficulty with the video-game generation. They are already able to distinguish between the frequent game users and the non-users among their pupils. To keep video kids attentive, teachers may condense their instructional material so that it gets to the point more quickly. With or without video-game experience, young children have notoriously short attention spans, which some teachers feel the games are shortening even further. "I feel I have to be entertaining in order to compete with computer games," one elementary school teacher said, expressing a sentiment echoed by others, some of whom resent being forced into changing their teaching styles. It is likely that this trend will continue as more children are exposed to home-computer games, and as educational video games become common in classrooms.

145

More broadly, it would be erroneous to conclude that occasional exposure to video games is turning children into little automatons. Teachers report that children still want time spent addressing personal and emotional issues. Students enjoy talking about their personal experiences, receiving the attention of an adult, identifying with characters in traditional stories. But more didactic activities seem to try the children's patience more than before.

The fantasy world created by a video game is unlike the imaginary one conjured up by a book or movie. Children can easily admit to being affected differently by a movie like Walt Disney's *Old Yeller*, in which a loyal dog is killed in an emotionally wringing final scene, and by a video game, whose "characters" are regularly annihilated without eliciting feelings from players. The games do promote a level of fantasizing—mostly involving destruction, conquest, or the winning of riches—but at heart the essence of the games is to rack up points. The fantasies of the games contain no genuine feelings. One young devotee of Space Invaders put it aptly: "Why should I care about the enemy? The point is to kill them." Children have always played at war games, and we accept as normal the urge to destroy make-believe enemies, be they human or alien. But through the intensity of the players' involvement, not to mention the sheer number of hours spent at play, video games reinforce more powerfully the children's disengagement from reality than do traditional games.

By and large, playing video games means obeying rules. Young video players, however, tend to prefer learning the rules of a game by playing it, not by listening to someone explain how to play. The latter takes too much time and attention. Moreover, as in solitaire, home video players like to be able to bend rules as needed.

> *Joanne (age 7):* The computer doesn't call you a cheater. It just makes noises. You can get away with more with the computer.

However, children, as a rule, detest making errors. They feel "mad" after they make mistakes. When doing homework, a child can erase mistakes, but "you can't reach into the video game and change things," as one child complained. Children generally feel pressure to improve their playing skills; mastering games is as important today as mastering baseball was in years past. One eleven-year-old commented, "Making an error makes me unhappy."

The video game has been praised by many as a model for educating children. Educational video games are supposed to make learning "fun and easy." But caution is advisable. The automatic quality of learning a basic skill on video may compete with learning other skills that require undergoing a certain amount of healthy frustration. It is important to consider what is appropriate developmentally for a child. For example, video games afford children a false sense of omnipotence. They come to believe that all their thoughts and actions are complete, perfect, and without challenge—like their control over the video world. There is a limit to how far this omnipotence should be reinforced. Furthermore, traditional games allow children to rehearse skills as well as to enjoy unfettered play.

146

Video games, however, are all rehearsal. Hours spent at video games are hours spent in highly restricted activity, and the amount of time spent creatively is cut down. This may impede the development of a child's imagination, just as connect-the-dots and coloring books without freehand drawing tend to teach control at the expense of creativity.

It is important to engage the fantasy life of children appropriately. Many fantasy stories allow children to think creatively about the world. Children's stories can be a way to teach ethical lessons to young children: what's cruel and what's generous, what's selfish and what's kind. Fantasy needs to be nurtured in the direction of a different possible life, one that is more human, not less.

True play—with its use of imagination, daydreaming, and fantasy—is beneficial to the developing child, as psychologists from Freud to Erik Erikson have known. Margaret Logan, writing in *Boston Review,* spoke for many when she questioned the effects of video games on children's creativity:

> With invention, fantasy, chance, and the hope of winning subtracted, only one of the elements of play is left: the impulse to create orderly form. The video machine obviously delivers order, in spades. The kid who achieves a degree of mastery . . . knows precisely when a belt of asteroids will swarm onto the screen and threaten his spaceship. The most complete mastery belongs to individuals most capable of submission to a machine's fixed program.
>
> Only a dedicated conspiracy theorist would believe that video machines are deliberately "designed" to promote habits of submission and spawn docile workers, voters, and consumers. Nevertheless, the machines' limited, canned programs will nurture few apostates, heretics, innovators, prophets, or conscientious objectors, . . . [those] imaginative spoilsports who refuse to obey the rules.

At a time when video games are pushing schools

147

toward more solitary learning exercises, it is important that we continue to pay attention to the social aspects of schooling. Cooperative skills are essential in adult life, and children need to practice them.

Teachers and parents have little to gain from banning video games altogether. These games can indeed be a useful adjunct to the classroom, for example, but teachers must spend time talking with children about the different learning media. Discussing the values of each and the importance of appropriate transitions from one form to another are a first step in helping children keep video games in perspective.

148

Despite the lack of research into the effects of video games on the way children think and behave, many people see them as a boon to American education as the nation's schools struggle to rise above a state of mediocrity. Some advocate using games as much more than a teacher's aid. Nolan Bushnell, inventor of Pong, founder of Atari, and the brain behind the Androbot home robot, told *Success* magazine of his plans for educational video arcades to which children would supposedly flock after school:

> I plan to be the technological Maria Montessori of the next three decades. . . . The system I would put together, if successful, would take an amount of strain off the public education system. Certain public systems will, in fact, copy my system—maybe even buy my system. I say, "God bless them." If it raises SAT scores, the public will demand it.

Computers are already accepted as a means of educating the young, and as the surge in computerized education builds, examination of its effects on children are urgently needed. Problems of the computer-centered home multiply in the computer-centered school. Small-scale domestic aberrations are becoming institutionalized.

Changes unfold so rapidly that they are difficult to evaluate.

"Schools are in the grip of a computer mania," *Popular Computing* magazine announced in a recent cover story. "In the past year or two, computer literacy has become a kind of political football at the federal, state, and local levels. No one quite knows what it is, but everyone is sure that it's good for us."

School departments traditionally move cautiously in adopting new teaching programs, and textbook publishers normally take years to develop, evaluate, and produce new textbooks. When it comes to acquiring computer hardware and software, however, schools and suppliers throw caution to the wind. Writes *Popular Computing*'s Dan Watt:

> Rather than slowing down and carefully examining their long- and short-term goals, school districts are scrambling for the latest technology, the most elaborate systems, and the lowest hardware prices without fully knowing what they are going to do with computers when they get them . . . although it is almost universally acknowledged that educational software is still in its infancy and that most available software is inadequate and unimaginative.

The signs of the computers-in-schools stampede are everywhere. From 1981 to 1982 the total number of schools with computer technology rose dramatically: 33 percent for high schools, 48 percent for junior high schools, and nearly double—85 percent—for elementary schools. Colleges such as Amherst and Smith offer interest-free loans and other special deals to students who want to buy personal computers. Clarkson College of Technology in Potsdam, New York, requires all freshmen to have computers. Drexel University in Philadelphia and Carnegie-Mellon in Pittsburgh will soon follow suit. Harvard plans to require computer experience for graduation.

The so-called Apple Bill has also helped feed comput-

149

ermania. Conceived by Apple Computer's Steven Jobs and pushed through the California state legislature in 1983, the Apple Bill allows for tax deductions for computers donated to schools by computer companies. This would, in effect, speed the flood of computers into classrooms. Apple quickly launched its own effort, called the "Kids Can't Wait" program, to donate an Apple computer system to every eligible public and private school in California. Keeping the ball rolling, the California legislature is now considering mandatory computer literacy for all high school graduates.

150

Clearly, the boom in school computers is not simply the result of an expressed need. Many of those calling for more and more computers seem unconcerned about just what they should be used for. Computers, it seems, are not a means to a particular end, but rather an end in themselves. Consider these comments by David Grady, a regular contributor to *Personal Computing* magazine:

> Apple's canny offer to donate computers to schools in return for a substantial tax write-off points the way toward a saner, healthier future for everyone. If we thought it important enough, we could flood the schools with computers and enlist both teachers and their students in the active search for things to use them for.

The degree to which the computer industry, the educational establishment, and spokespeople of all persuasions have pushed to create a need for computers is unique in the history of products. It may be inaccurate to say that everyone agrees about the universal benefits of computer literacy. Rather, the consensus seems to be that computer illiteracy is bad for us, for the underlying appeal of the sales pitch is simple: fear. Like those who flock to adult computer camps to learn how to "defend themselves" in the coming electronic civilization, students, teachers, and parents are responding to the computer industry's negative sell. Patricia Sturdivant, the new "associate superintendent for technology" of the two-hundred-thousand-student Houston school district, speaks for many other educators when she explains Houston's embracing of computers: "This is the wave of the future. We want our students to be able to survive out there in a world where technology will soon dominate."

As in the electronic workplace, the nature of this hard sell does not go unnoticed by teachers or students. The message is clear: adapt or perish. "Educational software has not yet arrived, as far as I'm concerned," observes software entrepreneur Thomas F. Snyder of Tom Snyder Productions. "Teachers are jumping onto the bandwagon from anxiety—they don't want to be left out." A senior at an inner-city high school told *The Wall Street Journal,* "Everything you see on TV—it's computer this and computer that. If it's going to take over, maybe I can get a job with one." The student's tone is one of resignation, not welcome. As George A. Miller, a psychologist at Princeton University, commented, "Schools are being asked to enable people to live symbolically. More and more, people will become useless if they cannot live at this symbolic level."

As the computer phenomenon gathers force in the nation's schools, reservations about how and how not to use them are swept aside. The thrill of discovery seems to be the goal: we'll buy the computers and then we'll figure out what to do with them. Behind much of the movement's momentum lurks that key attribute of the computer—speed. The computer promises faster learning, more efficient teaching. If we can teach children to read or to think logically at a younger age, why wait? We live in a world where activities and attributes that can be numbered, measured, or scored are always preferable. What many of us overlook is the difficulty in measuring things like "learning" and "comprehension," and the stresses that result when, having assigned values to these concepts, we seek "optimization."

Amid the race to acquire computers, there is anything

but consensus among educators as to how best to use them to teach. One popular development is computer-aided instruction (CAI), which critics say is nothing more than electronic flashcards, drilling pupils in basic skills such as spelling or multiplication tables, often unimaginatively. Defenders point out that CAI is an effective tool for raising the SAT score, that epitome of the quantification of wisdom. In less prosperous and progressive school systems, such as those of inner cities, this is often the only organized use of computers. A *Wall Street Journal* account described an Atlanta public school whose sole scheduled computer class was remedial reading:

152

> One eighth-grader, Tracy Love, describes her work this way: "The computer gives me a paragraph to read, I put an answer on my work sheet and the computer lets me know if I'm right or wrong." When she answers correctly, the computer screen fills up with little "wows."
> "The kids fall out of their chairs when they see that," says Linda Clements, a remedial-reading teacher.

After months of drill, however, it is unlikely that students will continue to fall out of their chairs from the novelty of it all. Eventually, filling in the blanks at a VDT begins to seem much like filling in the blanks in a workbook. "I've already seen this beginning to happen," one teacher told *The New York Times*. "If you want to teach the basics better, don't use computers; get older kids to teach younger ones."

In the poorer schools in general, computers are simply not as available to students as in the richer, more progressive schools. A study funded by the National Science Foundation found that "ominous inequities" continue to exist regarding computer opportunities in public schools. These inequities may, in fact, be worsening. Children in suburban and well-to-do urban schools were twice as likely to have had computer experience than were children in disadvantaged urban areas. Students in rural areas and in the southeast were also consistently less likely to have been exposed to computers in their schools. The upshot is that unequal computer availability will serve as a wedge driving advantaged and disadvantaged children further apart. In the words of Dr. Ronald Anderson of the University of Minnesota, who conducted the study:

> The implications are not just ethical and social, but they are economic as well. If differential opportunities for computer literacy continue to grow, large segments of the labor force will be rendered increasingly less productive as a consequence of not being able to function effectively and comfortably with the computers around them.

153

It is clear that computers can be an invaluable asset in education, and it is a healthy sign that schools everywhere are becoming aware of this. Still, we must make sure that our delight in the computer's possibilities does not overshadow what we have always valued in education: the human element, the teacher-student relationship. A good teacher is a role model and a caring source of encouragement and understanding. A computer is none of these. Some students like computerized math drills "because the computer doesn't yell at me," as one child said, but a good teacher doesn't yell either. A good teacher inspires pupils to explore subjects in new ways and with new enthusiasm, while a computer is "bland, faceless, and unresponsive," in the words of *New York Times* computer columnist Erik Sandberg-Diment. "I for one can't really accept it as a teacher," he writes. "The computer as presently programmed is too rigid, unforgiving, blatantly crude to be a good instructor. As a tool it may be neutral, as a teacher it is negative." A teenage computer user in California commented: "Teachers are sometimes better because they can understand your problems, whereas a computer just gives it to you straight. . . . You can't argue with a computer, if a problem is unfair or asks something you haven't learned about. It can't answer a question like a teacher."

Many computerphiles see computer programming, not canned software, as the key attraction of computers as an educational tool. To them, the computer is a tool for fundamentally reshaping the way children think. A central focus of these advocates is a computer language for children called LOGO, with which even kindergarten children can punch in rudimentary commands creating color graphics. Its devotees are often ecstatic in their praise. Brian Harvey, formerly the director of a high-school computer center in Lincoln, Massachusetts, wrote in *Byte* magazine recently, "LOGO is a language for learning. . . . To put it somewhat grandly, LOGO is a language for learning how to think." Herbert Simon, one of the leading lights in the artificial intelligence field, has even suggested that the meaning of the word "know" is changing from "having information stored in one's memory" to "the process of having access to information." In other words, it doesn't matter whether your brain can summon up the information, as long as you know how to access a database.

With this sort of mindset, we teach our children to think logically and sequentially. But once they stray outside the computer's world, they find their technical mastery irrelevant and their ability to communicate with others weakened. No one has proved that learning to write a good computer program helps a person behave with greater wisdom or reason in the real world. In fact, what is rational in a computer program—such as efficiency or brevity—can appear irrational when it guides one's relationships with others.

Most computer advocates cite as their goal the teaching of formal, mathematical logic—the earlier, the better. But according to many psychologists this is only one of nine cognitive styles that children develop, each style adding in its way to the child's development. Equal in importance to mathematical logic is synthetic thinking, in which

154

divergent thoughts are brought together to produce new wholes. Synthetic thinking is a creative mode of thought without which we would have neither art nor true science. MIT's Joseph Weizenbaum uses Newton's discovery of gravity as a famous example of synthetic thinking, since it was formulated by a fusion of "the contextual framework consisting of the behavior of everyday objects in the material world, like apples falling to the ground, with that of the solar system." Why should the learning of mere mathematical logic be accelerated to the detriment of these other skills? Do we need a world in which everyone is a superior programmer and not an artist or even a creative scientist? Sadly, in many schools the beliefs of computer advocates are being accepted without challenge; programs for art, music, social studies, and physical education are cut back so computers can be paid for.

155

Another stage of mental development in danger of neglect by an increasingly computer-oriented school system is dialectical logic, a way of thinking that involves not the simple accumulation of facts and skills but rather the ability to notice qualitative changes and appreciate the process of thought. According to psychologist Klaus Riegel, dialectical logic is the recognition of contradictions as a basic mode of thinking, a mode that mathematical logic rejects:

> Formal logic, if it could be carried consistently into concrete life situations, would leave [people] with long lists of possibilities and options, with many ifs and whens, but would not aid them substantially in reaching decisions and initiating actions.

The fact that most people learn how to shop in supermarkets is ample evidence that they have learned how to think dialectically. Implied in dialectical thought is what passes as common sense with its many judgments of value, as well as the ability to cope with the intangible, particularly in human interactions. It is this that the computer-touting educators would unwittingly school out of our children.

Many educators are computer boosters whose dreams for the computer seem to be without limit. Prominent among them is the inventor of LOGO, Seymour Papert, a professor of mathematics at the Massachusetts Institute of Technology. Papert foresees an end to a culture in which science and technology are alien to most of the population. In his book *Mindstorms: Children, Computers, and Powerful Ideas,* he discusses how computers can influence the way people think, "even when they are far removed from physical contact with a computer." Papert diverges from Piaget, his former teacher, in his emphasis on the role culture plays in a child's mental development. Piaget theorized that at certain predictable ages children begin to grasp new concepts intuitively, such as that when a toy is held behind one's back, it still exists but is only hidden. Papert, unlike Piaget, emphasizes the idea that tools can help hasten this natural unfolding of the child's innate mental stages. For example, in Papert's view the fact that so many important things come in pairs (hands, feet, parents) helps children develop their intuitive sense of number. He says,

> But in many cases where Piaget would explain the slower development of a particular concept by its greater complexity or formality, I see the critical factor as the relative poverty of the culture in these materials that would make the concept simple and concrete.

For Papert, our culture lacks "objects to think with," such as his Turtle, a computer-controlled cursor that children manipulate to draw pictures. He tells us that the Turtle "serves no other purpose than being good to program and good to think with." Children normally learn mathematical logic around age twelve, and Papert wishes to engineer them to learn it in half the time, to ease their passage from childhood to adulthood.

While acknowledging the potential effect that "a massive presence of computers and other interactive objects might have on children," Papert gives no hint that he understands the deeper psychological implications of this sort of accelerated learning. He admits to being warned that more computer communications might mean less human contact, but "despite these concerns I am essentially optimistic—some might say utopian—about the effects of computers on society." His technological bias is evident. Papert's focus is entirely on the individual child and his computer, on the "interactivity" of machine and child. Adults and other children in the environment, for example, are irrelevant to this.

Preschoolers, even infants, are not immune from the mad dash for computer literacy. An ad in *Parents Magazine* for a crib toy proclaims: "Fisher-Price introduces data processing for the beginner." Although the featured toy is designed to appeal to a baby's sense of touch and sight and to stimulate eye-hand coordination, the ad goes on: "Our activity center gives babies a vivid display of buttons to press, knobs to turn and more. . . . At first it's just trial and error. But soon baby figures out that to make the bell ring, you push the red button. He doesn't know it, but he's applying the scientific method." In a similar vein, one television commercial for a personal computer shows a parent and toddler "playing" with a home computer. Although he's only three, the announcer tells us, the child can benefit from the computer because it will "challenge, encourage and give him a headstart." The spiel's not-so-subtle clincher: "Don't put it off."

Papert may be contributing unwittingly to an increasing problem in our culture. In *The Hurried Child*, child psychologist David Elkind noted that today's pressures on middle-class children to grow up fast begin in early childhood. According to Elkind, "chief among them is the pressure for early intellectual attainment, deriving from a changed perception of precocity."

Children are put on the ski slopes as toddlers and are taught everything from violin to foreign languages before they enter first grade. They are expected to know how to take care of themselves at an early age. They are not allowed to pass through childhood at any natural pace; instead, they are constructed in the image of the adult—an image of perfected skills and abilities.

158

Elkind indicates that the negative consequences of hurrying our children may not show up noticeably until adolescence. In their search for identity, the rush to experiment with everything from drugs to sex leads young people into serious trouble because they are not emotionally prepared to handle these experiences.

Technostress in children will accentuate this process more than ever before, and at an even earlier age.

In general, those who champion the computer as a learning tool disregard the value of social relations in children's development. Two years ago the Center for Children and Technology in New York was "born of the need to bring thoughtful research to bear on burgeoning electronic technology and its role in children's lives." The center's primary interest was to study how planning skills develop, how children understand classroom work, and how they solve problems using computers. One study found "significantly more task-related interaction and collaboration when children worked on computers than when they worked on other classroom tasks. There was very little task-irrelevant talk when children worked with computers." The researchers' bias is readily apparent here. They have used an information-processing model for their research, without an attempt at qualitative analysis. They seem to ignore that "task-irrelevant" talk adds to children's problem-solving abilities by allowing them to interact in a nonfocused way, and that it gives children a chance to rest their minds while working on a problem.

Children, as we know from developmental psychology, have a need to play and socialize while they work. In fact, studies have shown that at early ages children need social interaction to carry out higher-order psychological processes such as problem solving. They learn from peers in a group or from adults who present them with opportunities to tackle something new or try a new approach to an old problem. They learn not only to accomplish the task but also to talk about their interaction with others. It is part of the elaborate social nature of children that is so exciting to watch as they explore their world.

Soviet psychologist L. S. Vygotsky, after studying children's mental development, concluded that "what children can do with the assistance of others might be . . . even more indicative of their mental development than what they can do alone." Vygotsky emphasized the role of social interaction in the development of all higher mental functions. Children learn to solve problems themselves most successfully if adults or more advanced peers keep them from getting sidetracked, suggest untried approaches, and offer encouragement. Children, in effect, learn to "think" with the help of sensitive, caring companions. The levels of communication between an adult and a child learning a new task are extremely complex. Trust, encouragement, and sensitivity to nonverbal cues are all important elements in this communication—elements that a computer would be hard pressed to provide.

As with adult users, children who focus their attention too narrowly on the computer and its procedures risk dimming their capacity to solve abstract problems and to appreciate the subtleties of human relationships. Papert has said approvingly, "The computer can make the most abstract things concrete." But what about abstract problems requiring abstract thought? How, using logic, can a child discover that he or she may have just hurt another's feelings and that an apology is in order? For that matter,

159

what good are adult friendships that are solely logical and concrete—the computer worker who comes home and "facts" with his wife, the network addict who logs on every night to consummate stimulating relationships? "Clear thinking" at an early age—or any age—should not be an unquestioned goal. There are too many realms of life and thought that "clear thinking" would leave no room for. MIT's Joseph Weizenbaum once designed as an experiment a computer program named ELIZA that could mimic a psychiatrist's end of a conversation; he was shocked when people suggested it might herald the beginning of cheap, automatic psychotherapy. Weizenbaum points out the danger of thinking we can reduce the world to discrete, analyzable chunks: "There's a whole world of real problems, of human problems, which is essentially being ignored."

160

Underlying the race to computerize the educational process is a deeper trend. An information-processing model of learning is gaining acceptance as the new educational norm. This model holds that the brain is essentially a data-processing computer. Knowledge and learning can be reduced to "effective procedures," much like a computer program. Children's brains should thus accept any data that are "formatted correctly." Schools have been on the defensive lately due to dropping student test scores and suspect teaching standards, and the information-processing model offers those institutions a way back to respectability.

It is important to understand that at the root of this model of education is the debate between humanist and behaviorist approaches to education that erupted in the 1960s. The behaviorists, led by B. F. Skinner, believe that when children learn, they are simply responding to external circumstances. The humanists, typified by Jean Piaget, believe that children have unique, essential natures and that regardless of external circumstances they will learn different subjects in different ways. That debate has shifted in the past ten years, and the behaviorists are being superseded by "cognitive psychologists," but their ideas are closely related. The cognitive psychologists advocate breaking down the learning process into a series of manageable steps. Goals for each step are set, and the child's performance in pursuit of those goals is measured. Teachers, in the same way, can be given a series of specific steps to follow in teaching reading, for example, so that the experience can be standardized and "quality controlled."

The cognitive psychologists, in promoting this brain-as-computer model, stress the advantages of speed, reliability, uniformity, and efficiency. Teachers and students can interact in specific predictable ways. Poor teaching can be controlled more easily because the teachers must no longer meet the demands of the humanist model, serving as a combination role model, entertainer, surrogate parent, psychologist, friend, and master of educational technique. Instead, the job of teaching can be, in effect, de-professionalized; one doesn't have to have years of experience or limitless insight in order to teach when one is following a comprehensive, step-by-step lesson plan.

Much of the debate occurs at universities and in academic journals. The full impact of the information-processing model has not yet had a chance to catch on in the nation's schools. But this does not make the subject an ivory-tower issue. What scientists and researchers in all fields are discovering and evaluating today have extremely rapid diffusion times. The silicon chip itself was invented barely fifteen years ago, and today it is one of the cornerstones of our world. New theories about differences in left-brain and right-brain learning were introduced only a few years ago; flight magazines now offer business managers tips on "right-brain management," and schools offer courses on drawing from the right side of the brain. Science today spreads so quickly that we must pay attention to what the theorists advocate. Already, cognitive psychologists expand their activities from exploring models of mental processes to advising educators about appropriate ways to teach. Teachers now use the information-processing model to teach children, which could well presage a new educational environment.

What is missing, however, is creativity. In place of humanistic values, a technocentered view of the world is reinforced. The essential battle is the battle for the brain. Once teachers decide that their pupils' brains are basically little computers, then we invite trouble. How we conceptualize our mental processes is crucial—as crucial as how we conceptualize our emotions.

*Reading and Understanding: Teaching from the Perspective of Artificial Intelligence,* a book written by Roger Schank of Yale's artificial-intelligence department, has been influential among cognitive psychologists. Schank, an early AI researcher, states his expertise in the area of teaching children how to read:

> Throughout most of my life, I have been involved in teaching computers to read. I have worked extensively on determining the nature of the human reading process, so that we could get computers to simulate it. I never thought a great deal about how children were taught to read. I assumed that it was being done in a reasonable fashion.

It is instructive to look at what Schank offers as reasonable, based on his experience with computers. In his book, he generalizes from adults to children. He asks the question: What do adults know that children do not? More specifically, he asks: What do adults know that enables them to read? One answer, of course, is orthography—young children don't know that a group of letters can indicate a word, or, if they do, they don't know what that word is. Schank goes on to discuss other, less obvious facets of knowledge that people need in order to read. He derives his list from AI research, "particularly with respect to the kinds of knowledge that computers need in order to understand stories." Computers must be able to:

1. make simple inferences;
2. establish casual connections;
3. recognize stereotyped situations;
4. predict and generate plans;
5. track people's goals;
6. recognize thematic relationships between individuals and society;
7. employ beliefs about the world in understanding it;
8. access and utilize raw facts.

163

Schank notes that "these eight kinds of knowledge roughly categorize what an adult knows about the world." He also notes that a child in the first grade has all this kind of knowledge, too, but in simplified form. He also says that "since reading depends upon this knowledge, effective reading instruction demands that we pay attention to this dependency." The eight types of knowledge that he has identified "help a reader to interpret what he hears, sees, reads, which in turn help him determine the impact of what he has read."

Schank attempts to demonstrate how the eight categories would apply to three-year-olds. He believes that after children have learned to recognize the words on a page, they should learn the fundamentals of comprehension. Not surprisingly, Schank finds that his eight categories of knowledge are the key to teaching children to comprehend what they read.

Given Schank's argument, one would assume that such logical categories are extremely helpful in teaching. The errors a child makes in trying to read a story, for instance, would presumably be corrected by dealing with whichever of the eight categories the errors occurred in. It all sounds very straightforward and worthy of adoption —until one looks at this approach a little more closely.

First, Schank fails to distinguish between the different ways in which children actually experience reading. In their book, *On Learning to Read,* Bruno Bettelheim and Karen Zelan (both of whom have years of experience teaching children to read, unlike Schank) identify two reading styles that vary from child to child and story to story: a child may read something in order to derive some sort of practical information from it—how to accomplish a task, or reach a destination, for example—or a child may treat reading as a source of open-ended knowledge and moving aesthetic experiences. It is significant that none of Schank's categories mentions anything about esthetics. Bettelheim and Zelan point out that the way or combination of ways in which children experience reading education depends on the impressions they receive from parents, the atmosphere of the home, and the way reading is taught in the school. In the formative years when children learn to read, they do not yet perceive things and activities on the basis of a rational and critical evaluation of their merit. Bettelheim and Zelan note that in order for literacy—the use of reading as a source of unlimited knowledge—to become the child's own goal, the child must endow it with highly personal meaning. They comment:

164

> To the modern educator, who views learning to read as the acquisition of a particularly important cognitive skill, it may seem a farfetched idea that this can be mastered well only if, initially and for some time to come, reading is experienced subconsciously by the child as a magic act, which potentially confers great and in some ways unknown powers. Yet it is the child's wish to penetrate what he believes to be the important secrets adults possess that makes learning to read an exciting adventure to him—one so attractive that he is eager to expend the requisite concentration and energy mastering it.

Schank never touches on such issues as emotion, magic, fantasy, imagination. He offers us logical categories that can be applied to children as well as adults. It fits the convenience of the adult, perhaps, but not the reality of the child.

Secondly, Schank assumes that children's errors are errors in logic, that somewhere within the eight categories lies the child's problem. The error should be located and a specific strategy applied to eliminate it. Teachers should help the child learn appropriate cognitive actions according to where the error lies.

Bettelheim and Zelan point to a study made in the late 1960s of reading errors made by first-graders:

> It was found that out of 1,943 ascertainable errors, 1,675—or 86 percent—were substitutions that made equal or better sense than the original text. [An example] is a child's reading "Spot can hear me" when his text was "Spot can help me." Spot is a dog, and a first grader knows that a dog can hardly help a child—but a dog can indeed hear the child and respond appropriately to his command.

According to this study, the next most common type of error was omission, which made up a little more than 6 percent of the children's errors. In these, children would skip a word that was part of the text, such as reading "the umbrella" for "the black umbrella." According to Bettelheim and Zelan, the study demonstrates that "nearly all errors made by the child being taught to read—whether he substitutes, omits, or inserts a word—either make the sentence more colloquial and less stilted or more sensible."

Anyone relying on a data-processing model of reading comprehension would, of course, be terribly frustrated by errors. They would want them corrected in a rapid and literal fashion. Not only would errors be seen as irritating, but they would also never lead to new information. Errors would tell us nothing about the individual child, only about how well the children are doing in each of the logical categories.

In a fascinating chapter entitled "Errors That Promote Literacy," Bettelheim and Zelan give an example of one third-grade girl who was preoccupied with feelings about her recent adoption. She was reading a book about a family that encounters British troops—"red coats"— during the Revolutionary War. The third-grader said "red coach" every time she saw the words "red coats," even after her teacher corrected her. The teacher concluded that the girl's error was not one of reading comprehension. Knowing that the girl had just returned from her first major vacation trip with her adoptive family, the teacher asked if by any chance they had stopped to eat at a Red Coach Grill (a popular east-coast restaurant chain). The girl replied that they had, and began to talk excitedly and in great detail about the experience, especially the all-you-can-eat feature, which she had never known about prior to her adoption. This explained the child's reading error: her recent trip was more exciting to her than the idea of en-countering red coats, and her mistake revealed her desire to talk about this emotion-filled experience. After talking about the reasons for her mistake with her teacher, the child was able to read "red coats" correctly.

In order to solve this child's error, the teacher had to bring a great deal of understanding and outside knowl-edge to bear on the child's reading experience. Moreover, the teacher had to tolerate the girl's initial error and use it to dig deeper into what the girl was really thinking about. The child benefited from the opportunity to talk about her feelings, and the teacher felt gratified by the challenge of unraveling the real reason for her pupil's problem.

Sensitivity and powers of observation like this are crucial attributes of a competent teacher. As the information-processing model of the brain gains accep-tance in education, however, there will be less freedom— or demand—for teachers to make use of these attributes. Scientific objectivity in the teaching of reading may actu-ally interfere with the teacher's ability to help chil-dren become literate in the best sense of the word.

166

Already there is a push to implement more computer simulations of reading skill weaknesses since a computer program could rate a child's reading level and point to strengths and weaknesses.

If this trend gathers force in the schools, the kind of sensitivity that Bettelheim and Zelan praise is certain to be undercut. Teachers concerned with meaning—paying attention not only to *what* children do but *why* they do it— are apt to be viewed as anti-progress. Furthermore, teachers will increasingly treat reading as simply another skill to be transferred, not a magical power to be conferred. This could bring about a generation of readers who are able to read material for little else but facts and instruction.

In addition, we risk letting our teachers downplay or shun their own skills if they begin to believe these skills are "fuzzy" and irrelevant from a cognitive-psychology view. We may even see those teachers who are slowest to encourage children's growth receiving the most recognition. The data-processing model of teaching is equivalent to the behavioral-objectives style of teaching of a few years ago. Now, however, the inner workings of the brain are at stake. We must move beyond the computer model and reveal it for what it is: another myth that limits our ability to explore the genuine richness of learning to be human.

# EIGHT

## Managing Electronic Space

"New problems mean new solutions."

*Alan*
Organizational psychologist

ELIMINATING TECHNOSTRESS is a cooperative venture. No single person or institution is the key to success. In the electronic workplace, no one has more influence in setting directions, of course, than the top brass. It is important that the chief executive officer and others in top management take an active part in shaping the role that computers will play in their particular operations. Leaving the implementation to middle management while merely monitoring the bottom line from a remote terminal is an unwise approach. Corporate policy filters down through management and ultimately influences the individual worker. Directives from the top dictate the speed and scale of computerization, the appropriate office behavior, and the hiring, promotion, and retention of employees.

Today, with companies investing more than ever in expensive new technologies, corporate policies must guard against pushing into the background the human needs and frustrations of the people using the technology. Whoever coined the term "employee subsystem" implied that human needs were a low priority in the structure of an office. But precisely because computers are so capital intensive and so central in a company's budgetary decisions, management must keep a sharp eye on how they are used. Technology that is poorly used represents a double financial burden. The machines' capabilities are wasted, and so are the workers' capabilities. Paying attention to human-centered objectives is therefore in the company's own best interests; an executive need not be "sentimental" to want to alleviate sources of technostress.

A key concern of any corporate chief is productivity, and when a company shifts to computerized operations its productivity depends on the speed with which its employees adapt to the new system. Long learning cycles can kill a new system. By the time production has been brought up to speed, much has been lost. If learning a new system is tedious and the workers uncomfortable, the technology may never be used effectively. If a word processor is used only as a typewriter, or a desktop computer as a calculator/calendar, the investment in computers is wasted.

171

Top management can avoid this kind of waste by implementing a consistent, humane policy spelling out how the new technology should be used. The policy should recognize the psychological needs of employees by taking into account the nature and content of their assigned tasks. The company must match jobs to people, rather than the other way around. Above all, the company must recognize and plan for the process of adaptation that people will go through.

An appropriate corporate policy should allow for differences in information processing capabilities among workers. The policy should encourage middle managers and supervisors to trust the employees' own perceptions of what they can and cannot accomplish. This means that managers must learn to accept the idea that there are limits to how much a worker can do at a terminal; too often, they notice that they are pushing their staff too far, too fast only when their employees begin to rebel. Employees ought to be allowed to decide for themselves when they need a break. The old fifteen-minute scheduled morning coffee break is no longer enough—if it ever was—given the intensity of computer work.

Similarly, companies must not allow the new computer setup to increase supervisors' control over employees by monitoring keystrokes or calling in workers for weekly or monthly "productivity reviews" based on computer tabulations. Rather than emphasizing a minimum amount of work a technical worker should do, a more enlightened policy would spell out a maximum—no more than three hours at a computer terminal at one stretch, perhaps, or six hours in one day. Coffee breaks and starting and ending times should not be scheduled by company fiat, but worked out cooperatively between employers and employees. This can serve to lessen the psychic drain that overcontrolled workers feel.

172

A good management policy would advocate a balance between productivity and worker well-being. This is sound policy for any company, but it is all the more crucial in computer work because the tendency toward imbalance is exacerbated in electronic space. An integrated human being requires challenge as well as rest, focused activity as well as relaxation. Workers suffering from eye strain, for example, should be provided with varying tasks; they can choose to do phone work, for example, when their vision begins to blur from reading the VDT screen.

IBM's model of the "WP Center" with its administrative secretaries and word-processing secretaries, by contrast, is a perfect example of what not to do. Individual needs are overlooked when a company subdivides all the variety out of the job; each typist typing and each programmer programming eight hours a day, five days a week. The original idea of division of labor was that each task would be performed by the person best qualified to do it. In the case of spot welders or electricians, this makes sense. Computers, however, are designed these days to make a variety of once-specialized jobs within reach of different workers. Why then separate administrative secretaries from word-processing secretaries?

In setting company policy regarding the entry of computers into the workplace, management should build a degree of challenge into every job. The mind revolts against work that is too simple, as it does against work that is too complex. Management should push to develop a genuine learning environment the moment an office introduces new technology. Jobs are redefined across the board and work relationships are redrawn. As legible handwriting, high mathematical aptitude, even good spelling diminish in importance, once out-of-reach tasks now are accessible to less-skilled workers, and this opportunity should be exploited to add variety to job descriptions.

Jobs can be made more challenging if workers are asked to contribute to the business enterprise as a whole, whether through regular discussions with management, redesigned work flows, or regularly scheduled learning and training sessions. Cutting workers off from the purpose of their daily tasks is a sure route to employee dissatisfaction.

173

As part of job redefinition, management should encourage people who don't normally work together to meet and share information. For example, when personal computers are brought into a work unit in a large office, a senior systems analyst is assigned to make sure that the project gets off the ground smoothly. But a professional analyst only sees one piece of the puzzle, and should consult with someone from the personnel or human resources department who is more accustomed to thinking in terms of human problems. Typically, neither the sellers or buyers of new computers want to point to any potential problems in implementing the system: both have a stake in its success. A company psychologist or manager of human resources can view the situation from a broader perspective, drawing attention to human factors. Computer experts should not necessarily dictate to future computer users precisely how and why they will use the new equipment; rather, it is essential that the workers themselves be consulted, whether or not they have any familiarity with computers. As well, pains should be taken to avoid the condescension with which many computer-literates address their less literate colleagues. Computer literacy is relatively easy to come by; hard-earned job experience is a good deal harder to attain. The skills of workers who are not computer-literate should be respected and taken into consideration when the office structures are revised.

Finally, a company policy should acknowledge employees' concerns and complaints about the new technology. This is a way for top management to let middle management know that the policy is a serious attempt to improve the quality of working life. Without explicit support from above, worker-oriented managers often feel that they lose ground to their technology-oriented counterparts. The latter are often regarded as the fastest-rising climbers on the corporate ladder. In reality, they may be doing more harm than good because they increase the potential for technostress in the ranks. This state of affairs can cause good people to leave and reduce the productivity of those who stay. Forced productivity produces short-term results—and long-term deficits.

James Robinson III, then chairman of American Express Company, wrote in *Chief Executive* magazine in 1981 that top executives must involve themselves when their companies computerize, predicting that "the morale and productivity of companies in the next decade may very well hinge on how well organizations ease employees' fears about new technologies and the dislocations they will bring to the workplace." As Robinson observed, perhaps we should worry less about managing machinery and worry more about managing the people who manage the machinery.

Middle management has a much more intimate view of technostress than does top management, as well as a more direct opportunity to prevent or at least alleviate it. The key for middle managers and supervisors is to abandon the idea that productivity is a measurable quantity and that the manager's job is simply to increase it. They should learn to encourage imagination, creativity, and innovation as well as output.

In human-oriented workplaces, managers avoid dividing and subdividing jobs excessively. Limiting workers to small functions leads to the notion of "stupid work." For example, managers sometimes view jobs that require only information processing as requiring little intelligence.

This is a version of the idea that the brains are in the planning department and the brawn is on the assembly line. Enlightened managers realize that jobs are only as stupid as they are set up to be. One bank manager, for instance, had always looked down on tellers as low-skilled workers with little to contribute. A consultant persuaded him to let the tellers meet with a systems analyst to suggest changes in the software they were using. The opportunity for making suggestions not only improved the tellers' morale but also led to improvements in the system, and convinced the manager of their worth to the bank.

In computer work generally, there is no reason that users, programmers, design personnel, and information processors should be split into four unconnected groups. Managers need to understand that if people learn to work together in new ways, the work environment as a whole can benefit. Cross-fertilization of ideas can lead to useful new approaches to problem-solving.

How to build a balanced environment that promotes individual learning while benefiting the organization is a key question for the business manager. The opportunity to learn is a potent attraction, and companies must begin to realize this. We are naturally inquisitive; we want to find out more about our world, about what makes things tick. Increasingly, employees are attending evening school and workshops of all kinds. They want depth to their inquiries. If a presentation or seminar is too thin on details and cases, they turn off mentally. We seek the stimulation of learning throughout our lives; the idea that we learn quickly only as children conflicts with the findings of developmental psychology. The very adaptability of the human brain makes us lifelong learners (although our response times to stimuli may slow down as we age). It is common today for middle-aged people to change careers, and many women have made the transition from the household to the business world, learning new skills as well as new ways of perceiving themselves and others.

Learning is an individual matter. Some people learn

better alone, others in groups; some in small steps, some with generalities. Some prefer to be confronted with the full brunt of reality; others like to be talked with gingerly. Conceptual thinkers learn differently from practical thinkers. There are as many combinations of learning styles and rates as there are fingerprints.

Managers in computer environments need to manage learning cycles. They must take into account individual responses to computers in order to accelerate and improve learning. By doing so, they can prevent the perceptual obstacles and mismatches that cause technostress.

Before computers are actually brought into an office, managers should meet with employees in small groups and discuss apprehensions they have about the changeover. Too often, the introductory meeting is a lecture by a sales representative of the computer vendor about the specific features of a new computer system, merely a summary of the user's manual. Employees, knowing nothing about computers, are confused by the sales rep's memorized rundown of computer functions, but don't know what critical questions to ask to clarify the presentation—and sense that they are not expected to ask. Meetings should be kept small and informal, with discussion of anxieties and impressions encouraged, however illogical they may seem. A group leader with some knack for leading discussions—someone who is more educator than technician—should guide the meeting with the basic assumption that new learning generates new problems as well as new challenges. The leader might initially ask what problems people expect the computers to create for them—a reduction in skill level, perhaps, or isolation from one's co-workers. Discussions might then center around the actual work of the office. The expectations of workers are crucial because so often they are self-fulfilling; an employee expecting difficulties usually has them. Problems and misgivings should be listed in order of importance on a board, and discussed.

Next, the discussion leader might encourage employees to list personal fears on paper. The papers are then gathered—no names required—and their contents listed on a blackboard. The number of mentions of each fear (or category thereof), such as fear of being unable to learn the new technology, is counted. Again, concerns should be rank-ordered and discussed in turn. The leader should then encourage discussion among the employees; this can help build small teams of people who can later help each other when adaptation begins.

Following this discussion, people might break up into small groups and rehearse the three or four predominant anxieties. They can do this through role-playing: one person takes the part of the harried worker trying to plow through an undecipherable user's manual, another plays a manager who is skeptical about the worker's frustrations. The role-playing sessions can help people step outside their personal fears and see them in more objective terms. This should lead into a discussion of strategies to counter the fears, after which the employees order and discuss possible strategies. Managers should pay careful attention to these constructive comments, choosing those that can be acted on once the computers arrive. For example, discussion groups may agree that a free tutorial class be offered to computer-shy workers; this might simply be an informal gathering led by a computer-literate coworker during company time. Managers should also take pains to address employees' negative expectations of how work is to change, perhaps by spelling out explicitly how current skill levels will be maintained or improved. This entire process can be done quickly, and is immensely more effective than placing machines in an environment and simply letting people learn haphazardly.

There is a world of difference between the preliminary, "expectation" phase of computerization and real hands-on experience. When actually faced with a computer, employees who had not worried much about the coming change or who had welcomed it may find adaptation difficult. Once their jobs are altered, fear and anger may surface. The hands-on experience is critical because it determines how people handle later learning in the event that the technology is updated.

In this initial learning phase, managers can help limit problems in several ways. With a cognitive learning test, for example, workers can better understand how they process information and where they might get into trouble. A person who uses a synthetic style of thinking, as mentioned earlier, may resist moving step by step through an operations manual or a tutorial designed for a software package, preferring to jump ahead in the exercise. Managers can intercede by stressing the idea that those having difficulty reading a user's manual, for example, are not slow-witted but perhaps simply unaccustomed to sequential thinking. Then an overview of the project that needs to be accomplished can be put together, before turning to the details involved in carrying it out. When workers find out how their thinking style influences their learning, they sometimes feel as though the proverbial lightbulb has flashed on above their heads. Learning becomes more rewarding, and they are encouraged to continue to think flexibly and imaginatively.

It is important that managers regulate the amount of work delegated to employees while they learn the technology. Nothing fuels more resentment among workers than learning computer skills while trying to manage a high workload. Employees interpret this, often accurately, as management insensitivity.

Management has several options. They can hire temporary help to take up some of the normal workload for a short period of time; this often works well and frees people to concentrate on their new tasks. Managers can also identify those workers who are doing well with the computers and have them help others who are not. This ameliorates feelings of helplessness and inability to learn and allows the learning to be informal and unpressured. It also builds a community of mutually supportive learners. Managers should understand that an employee/coach will have less time to devote to his or her regular tasks and that during this stage productivity is expected to drop; otherwise, the tutors will resent being pulled away from their normal tasks, and this will become painfully clear to the people they are tutoring.

Some companies who have understood this process have provided employee groups with video cameras to record the process of adaptation. These tapes are used to stimulate discussions of how well employees are coping with their problems. The videotapes are passed around to other groups so that they can see what others went through. This also allows managers to build a store of information about advances and setbacks in adaptation among employees. Most managers, at this point, have no training data to draw upon. Relying on informal observations and suggestions is too casual a way to evaluate the situation. When possible, a company psychologist or human-resource manager should examine the videotapes, or use other methods to document the adaptation process. This sort of qualitative analysis can feed back into future introductory meetings as a guide for discussion.

Once computers are in use throughout an office, the amount of conversation among employees tends to drop. They concentrate more on specific tasks, react to increased workloads, and become preoccupied with learning more about the system. This disrupts office friendships, informal patterns of sharing information, and relaxed time to chat with others. A decrease in general chatter may delight the old-school manager, but in fact it exacerbats the new danger of technostress and its long-term problems. Managers should encourage employees to continue their old lines of informal relations, perhaps by structuring time for people to meet informally to talk as they did prior to the introduction of the computers. This is not wasted time; it is time people need to rejuvenate themselves, check ideas and work-related thoughts, and build group identification.

The key to successful ongoing operations is no mystery. Management must plan for and design structures to accommodate high performance without technostress. Structuring time for employees to meet is the first move toward creating human-oriented work conditions. In computer environments, work design is critical. Design means more than formulating a plan to meet a specific end. It means building a flexible structure that promotes a balance between people and technology. The design of work itself can be perceived in terms of how people and jobs fit together. Several dimensions must be taken into account:

180

> *Knowledge:* Are workers' skills being fully used in their present jobs? Is their work sufficiently challenging? Do they want more opportunity to learn new things?
>
> *Psychology:* Are workers receiving sufficient recognition? Are needs for achievement being met? Is there room for advancement?
>
> *Efficiency:* Is the work exhausting? Is the degree of accuracy required excessive? Is sufficient information provided for maximum job effectiveness?
>
> *Task structure:* Is there sufficient variety in the work? Are workers given enough scope to use their own initiative? Are they provided with a chance to make planning suggestions?
>
> *Ethics:* Does management look after the interests of its employees? Do managers convey respect for the skills of the workers? How do workers perceive top management and its goals?

Most managers are locked into a mechanistic attitude about their employees' jobs. On the most basic level of production they see machines and people processing information. They try to control such variables as error rates, coffee breaks, and socializing of employees by setting up production schedules and quotas and insisting that they be met.

Managers who have not developed beyond the traditional industrial model of the workplace tend to welcome automatic error-monitoring systems. Unfortunately, using a machine to monitor error rates may keep those rates high. Workers resent feeling controlled by technology and overcontrolled by management. This creates hostility, which in turn generates more errors. One could, with proper knowledge, just as easily have the person work as a member of a group that monitors its own mistakes. This increases the cohesion among workers and reduces overall errors. People in this situation see themselves as responsible members of a group, and this perception encourages them to improve.

The next aspect of work to be structured is the flow of information. Where does it actually go? Is it used for decision-making? What strategies grow out of the information once it is received? It is essential that information be targeted to the appropriate person. Misdirected information renders the entire system useless, no matter how sophisticated. Just as inefficient is covering all bases by sending information everywhere. Managers in one department don't need to know how much stationery another department bought that month, nor do they want to be saddled with distributing the same information themselves. There is no substitute for a careful evaluation of information flow within a company—regularly assessing who should receive what, how important various types of information are, and what different employees actually need to know to carry out their tasks. Managers should develop ongoing information checklists and discuss them among themselves.

Along with the flow of information, the form it takes should be carefully considered. How is the information transmitted? Should recipients call it up on their VDTs as needed, or receive a printout? Is the layout of the words and figures easy to read? All too often, information goes to the right person, who then finds it unreadable. Columns of figures may be poorly arranged, or groupings or charts too time-consuming to interpret. The result is disuse, aggravation, and headaches. As more information becomes available to computer workers, ease in reading and use becomes critical. There are many ways to use information. To do so thoughtfully and creatively, we must be able to absorb it without a struggle.

The quality of our thinking—a most valuable resource—should not be tied to results alone, but nurtured as a process. Employees throughout a company should be encouraged to think critically, to question methods and even goals, and to suggest alternative ways of doing things. Increased choice allows the worker to transcend the immediate constraints of a problem and go beyond the information given. As Alexander the Great demonstrated when he untied the Gordian knot with his sword, generating alternatives is a matter of perception. The ability to perceive alternatives can be taught, and it is the responsibility of management to encourage this, through seminars, brainstorming sessions, imaginative work design, and, above all, flexibility.

Managers can work together as a group to devise alternatives to the traditional work model. Initially, they must pay attention to apparent surface contradictions in the workplace: computer users with a high level of skill and knowledge who remain bored and unchallenged; workers who suffer from isolation in their work, despite the increasing possibilities of working with others in new ways; workers who don't make use of the unprecedented amount of information at their fingertips. Once managers are willing to think about these contradictions, they often find that new solutions appear. Most managers are accustomed to playing the devil's advocate by finding flaws in what staffers propose. This is an essentially negative skill. By exploring contradictions in search for positive alternatives, we can move beyond approaches that are unconstructive, overly cautious, one-dimensional, and tradition-bound.

Once managers recognize contradictions, they should

182

list and discuss them among themselves and with their employees. The goal should be to recombine elements of the situation to create new strategies that eliminate the old contradictions. A strategy must take into account the entire situation, not just the most immediate problem. It should allow a step back to look at how the problem is influenced by a tangle of other relationships. Proposed strategies must then be tested against reality. Perceived contradictions in the new approaches should be pointed out and explored, and proponents of a particular strategy should try to remain open-minded and flexible. This is a cycle of thinking and rethinking the solutions to problems, to be viewed as a process that spirals forward, not as a treadmill of endless solutions that lead nowhere. The key is in the process as well as the solution.

As the computer is used for more analytic and synthetic activities, the assumptions upon which a software program was written become a key factor in understanding the solution to a problem. A program with weak assumptions will help generate an answer, but it may be off-target. "Meta-problem solving"—solving problems about problems—is playing an increasingly important role in the computer world. Managers must hold discussions on the assumptions that went into the programs they have purchased. When users don't trust a program—not an unusual occurrence—something is probably amiss with its assumptions. This takes the discussion of a solution to another level of abstraction. For this reason, flexibility and imagination become all the more important in evaluating old strategies and evolving new ones.

To deal with these issues, managers must place a high degree of trust in the workers they supervise. They must have a great deal of personal security and a sense of their own fallibility. To ask questions, expose contradictions, and model strategies, managers and employees alike must be sensitive to each other and open to constructive criticism.

To reduce the conditions that foster technostress,

managers need to design transitions that go beyond mere coffee breaks and respites from the terminals. Employees should be given an opportunity to sit down with others face to face to discuss their work, walk through the work unit to get a feel for what others are doing, and work with actual empirical models in order to regain a tangible feel for a computer-oriented project. Transitions should include significant noncomputer work; rotation of personnel can be beneficial all around. Systems designers can spend time talking with users, inside and outside the company, about what the latter face in their everyday tasks. For useful rotation to occur, management must learn to schedule workers' time in ways that are more open-ended and less tightly supervised than is traditional. This gives personnel the breathing room to think about their work from a fresher and more comprehensive perspective.

184

Transitions are particularly important at the end of the day. The computer-involved worker who leaves a terminal at five o'clock may appear tense and disoriented on arriving home shortly thereafter. An end-of-the-day breather, on company time, helps the computer worker shift contexts and leave unfinished problems at work where they belong. Because technical workers so often lose track of time, it is important that management take the responsibility for discouraging computer work after, say, 4:30 P.M. Some enlightened companies now provide time and facilities for employees to exercise and socialize, or simply let computer workers leave the office early to exercise on their own.

A more direct approach to combating technostress is an invitation to a professional counselor, perhaps to lead discussion groups for those who are having difficulty in making the transition to computerized work. A half-hour meeting might suffice, just enough time to let workers experience something different, think about computers from a new perspective, and relax. It might well head off a great deal of exhaustion and anxiety and help limit technostress. Professional counseling can also be utilized on a

much larger scale. At a number of forward-thinking corporations, management has begun to appreciate the role psychologists can play in the production process. With so
many companies in recent years plagued by falling productivity and employee turnover, more and more have begun
to look beyond the efficiency expert for ways to improve
the production process. Organizational psychologists are
now brought in to discuss employee problems with
workers and managers on a regular basis, either through
departments of human resources or as outside consultants. Psychologists research such factors as work station
design, train managers to deal with employees more effectively, and, most important, supply theories about human
development to organizations concerned about their employees' productivity and well-being.

Most such organizational psychologists have a clinical orientation toward their work. They strive to improve
worker motivation, reduce occupational stress, and
heighten the sensitivity of managers toward their personnel. The clinical orientation is undeniably useful. It has
emphasized important individual factors in the success of
organizations, and the work lives of managers and workers alike have benefited.

Some organizational psychologists realize, however,
that behavior within an organization is more complex than
is commonly believed. For motivation to improve, for example, a change is needed not only in employee attitudes,
but also the nature of the work they perform. The psychologist must be a sociologist and business analyst as
well. This change in orientation should not be under-
estimated. It views behavior as inseparable from the work
environment, and thus encourages attention to the human
needs of employees in balance with business objectives.

It is essential that organizational psychologists
become familiar with the special problems of electronic
space so that they can play an active rather than reactive
role in its design and management. In this era of occupa-

tional specialization, the psychologist's expertise must be interdisciplinary to meet the challenge of technostress.

The key area of attention must be the manner in which the new technology is introduced to a workplace. For too long this has been left to systems engineers who draw up elaborate diagrams indicating target dates, areas to be computerized, and suggested work flows—with no regard to the workers who must adapt to these systems. As a result, it is not unusual for the most well-designed systems (from the systems-engineering point of view) to fall apart once people try to work within them.

186

Before implementation, organizational psychologists should evaluate current operations so that computerization does not take place in departments already suffering from morale problems. It makes little sense to force new learning requirements on workers already plagued with problems. This mistake usually occurs when management adds a computer system to a work group whose productivity has dropped; the managers figure they can turn the situation around by firing a few employees and letting the computerized system force the others to work more productively. To forestall such a calamity, psychologists should actively participate in the design of any implementation program. As part of this process, they should hold pre-implementation meetings with employees to discuss the latter's concerns about the coming change. When the system is put into operation, regular meetings should continue so that complaints, fears, resistances, and uncertainties can be aired. Typical subjects might be the changes in the way workers will be required to cooperate with one another, or aspects of their old jobs that the workers would like to see carried over into their new jobs.

The emerging field of ergonomics describes many of the interdisciplinary elements to which the organizational psychologists must pay attention. Ergonomics, literally the study of work, usually refers to the dynamics of "man-machine interface," the way machines can best be designed to accommodate their human users. A growing cadre of professionals from a variety of fields, from mechanical engineering to interior design, now refer to themselves as ergonomists.

To be sure, ergonomists often add useful knowledge to the debate over what makes for a successful union of user and machine. Unfortunately, their perspective is often too narrow. Gunnor Borg, a research psychologist at the University of Stockholm, has summarized the problem: "To better understand man at work . . . speed and error of performance should be complemented not only by physiological measurements of strain and work load, but also by measurements and indicators of the third main effort continuum: the perceptual." Borg points out that ergonomists have tended to underplay the actual human costs of operating new technologies.

Since most supervisors and managers view the man-machine interface only in terms of how productive the worker will be in the short run, psychologists must help them see the importance of qualitative factors to productivity in the long run—factors like purpose, pride, support, independence, and self-esteem. An important ingredient in quality work is effective communication, and pyschologists must teach managers how to listen.

People and production alike are constrained when managers assume that there is one best way to introduce a new technology and reorganize tasks. Managers must not rely on designers who talk in terms of optimal procedures and other abstract concepts that don't take into account the way people actually work, with all their imperfections, limits, preferences, and strengths. Instead of using so many mathematical assumptions, formulas, and strategies, managers would be better off using a phenomenological approach to discover how people perceive their work—which tasks are more or less interesting, demanding, or redundant—and how workers contribute to the job beyond what is written in their job description. It is the responsibility of the organizational psychologist to press for recognition of this view.

Another set of problems is arising that requires the psychologist's attention—boundary problems. These occur at a point where one work unit must cooperate with another; where production staff meets with marketing staff, for instance. The traditional problem, from a psychological perspective, is that those at the boundaries suffer stress from acting as go-betweens for often conflicting interests. The role calls for diplomacy, negotiating skills, and flexibility, though management often does not recognize this. Friction at the boundaries within an organization becomes more intense in the computerized environment. Part of the problem is that as information flow accelerates, boundaries multiply. The centralization that computers bring requires that data processors or programmers provide services to more and more disparate departments. As a supervisor of a financial planning program at Barclay's Bank put it, "My support group is located in Los Angeles. I have to continually work with them to keep the program functioning and work with my boss to see that people are using and relying on the program. I talk to people in L.A. that I've never met. Sometimes I feel that my boundaries are all over the place."

A manager of information services for a San Francisco department-store chain cited another aspect of this new boundary problem: "I'm responsible for seeing to it that the information needs of the company are kept current. I manage everything from accounting to inventory information. The information is what I identify with. . . . I don't really feel an allegiance to people, jobs, or sometimes even the company—just the information."

Such workers feel lost in the welter of new and thus poorly defined relationships. They feel uncomfortable moving about the company, like the information they generate, without any real attachments. This dissatisfaction presents a new area of research for organizational psychologists. It is precisely because today's electronic workplace has no real antecedents that the workers have no behavioral model on which to rely. The knowledge worker has come a long way from the days of the hereditary crafts and guild apprenticeships; new solutions to new problems must be found, and the observations and analyses of organizational psychologists must be an essential part of this search.

Psychologists of the workplace bear a great responsibility to those affected by computerization. They must help those in management think in a flexible way—a Herculean task, by all indications. They must impress upon management the notion that computers are potent, and that the human consequences of this must be recognized. Psychologists with an understanding of the risks of technostress will fight an uphill battle over the next few years, or longer —as long as technical personnel maintain their stronghold on the design and implementation of computer systems. But, at the risk of being labeled "sentimental," organizational psychologists must accept responsibility for pushing for more humanistic strategies within the corporate culture. In the long term, everyone will benefit.

It would be wishful thinking, of course, to expect all corporate planners and managers to utilize outside help and to involve employees in decision-making. In general, companies need prodding if they are to behave progressively. This is where unions can play a helpful role in heading off technostress.

Traditionally, unions have concentrated on blue-collar industries. Although they have succeeded in winning many important concessions for industrial workers—from appropriate break times to on-site areas for rest and relaxation—unions have tended to be reactive, not imaginative. Only when conditions are blatantly bad are they likely to fight for improvement.

More and more now, unions are moving into white-collar areas, and it is vital for them to understand the special problems of "knowledge workers," and technostress in particular, if they are to be influential. Unions are now seeking agreement from management on such new issues as job boredom. In the Boston area, the working women's organization, 9to5, has lobbied for a contract clause in which companies accept the idea that "routinization of the secretarial profession through the introduction of new technological changes is undesirable."

Because computerization affects an office so drastically, unions can play a role in making sure that change is used as an opportunity for betterment, not an excuse for making menial jobs even more menial. Retraining guarantees are a key part of this effort. Rather than trying to block automation, unions can seek to increase job mobility by ensuring that workers get a chance to upgrade their skill levels and receive on-the-job or company-subsidized training for new jobs. The Service Employees International Union (SEIU) has been active in organizing electronic-office workers. Sample contract provisions it advocates include job rotation (giving VDT operators the opportunity to switch to non-VDT work during the day) and rest breaks (a fifteen-minute break every two hours, and never a full day at a VDT).

Unions must take a more constructive and less defensive stand if they are to play a meaningful role in shaping the workplace of the future. Unions need to accept the fact that computers are here to stay, and should begin exploring how workers can benefit from this. For example, unions could organize workshops on a creative use of computers or on new career opportunities available as a result of new technology. Workshops like these should examine the psychological areas of people's work lives. They key is not simply to fight battles over power, but to empower people by helping them expand their ideas of what is possible. There is a great potential among workers to create a genuinely different future, and unions can play a more active role in encouraging their professional development.

# NINE

## Closing the Generation Gap

"In the classroom or at home, it's still how you relate to a child that matters—not what gadget you show them."

*David*
Parent

PREVENTIVE MAINTENANCE is always preferable to emergency repairs. Many of the dangers of technostress can be circumvented if we begin to pay attention to ways in which our children can learn to use technology without losing their perspective. Healthy adaptation to computers when they are in school is easier to manage and more likely to be successful than sending them to therapists when they are adults.

Teachers, of course, play a pivotal role in determining this adaptation. With an awareness and understanding of technostress and its sources, they can do much to make sure their students do not begin to show an unhealthy relationship to computer technology. Too few school systems seem particularly worried about the problem. With schools nationwide facing accusations of mediocrity, educators and parents look to computers as a cost-effective key to the future. (Not everyone is happy with the emphasis on cost-effectiveness. A cartoon in the San Francisco *Chronicle* depicted a coin-operated robot seated behind a desk in front of a class. Behind it on the blackboard were the words, "Hello. I am your substitute teacher. For 10 minutes of education, please deposit 10 cents.")

Teachers face the largest reorientation of the classroom ever. Urged on by hardware and software companies, parents, and local school boards, they are faced with adapting as quickly as possible to computers in the classrooms. Many teachers risk the effects of technostress themselves and must live a double life: persuading their students to learn to use computers while secretly questioning their value.

To maintain their equilibrium, teachers would do well to learn about the computer until they are able to master the level of knowledge expected from their students. Wise teachers do not ask their students to learn what they themselves have not mastered. Teachers should take time to determine the relationship of computers to their own learning experiences and needs. Even if they assume that computers are the "wave of the future" and that students must be "prepared for the real world," teachers should be able to identify clearly the educational costs and benefits presented by the technology. As well, teachers should pace themselves in their adaptation to computer use, and not jump on the bandwagon or reject computers out of hand. It takes time to integrate a new tool system into well-established patterns of teaching and learning.

Before teachers begin to experiment with computers in a classroom, they need to consider educational values, to examine the ideas and ways of thinking that are most worthy of being passed on to students. It is clear, for instance, that computer-aided instruction—the use of computers essentially as electronic flashcards, as for multiplication drills, touch-typing lessons, or SAT practice—can be effective. However, it is important to question the value of accelerating a child's facility at the expense of creativity. A teacher may want students to discern the message of a story or to judge the difference between two sets of social values. Here, computer-aided instruction is of little use.

Some computer advocates say that the time saved by computer-aided instruction makes room for other kinds of learning. This is not necessarily the case, however; the emphasis on rote and gimmick may crowd out the joy of learning, the acquisition of genuine literacy, and the development of a child's sense of self. Teachers need to consider whether it is true education if a highly intelligent young person seems headed toward an adulthood with an

193

unintegrated emotional life. They need to question their definition of an "educated person." Certainly, education should add to a person's maturity, not merely provide an ability to solve problems.

New computer programs are placing greater power in the hands of educators. Early types of computer-aided instruction were little more than unimaginative multiple-choice tests, and because the mental effort required was minimal, students remained uninterested. There was little likelihood that they would prefer computers to teachers. However, the sophistication of programs in the last few years has improved remarkably. Stunning graphic images, brilliant color, variable response times, and interactive programs that change according to the user's skill draw the student in.

Teachers must learn how to assess the software they use in teaching children. It is irresponsible for teachers to leave such choices to an administrator. One software package may have brighter colors, but its exercises may be dull and unimaginative. Teachers must ask themselves whether the students will be sufficiently challenged. They should work up a model of evaluation that suits their needs, judging software according to set criteria; ideally, they should encourage the students themselves to learn to judge the pros and cons of new software packages.

What is needed is more understanding of how the findings of developmental psychology can be turned into guidelines for classroom instruction. Allan Gould, an educational psychologist at the University of California at Berkeley, has suggested that teachers might ask the following questions, among others, as they begin to develop new teaching programs:

1. What is the goal of the instruction? Is it to teach a skill that is developmental in nature and thus unsuitable for children under a certain age?

2. What alternatives are available for teaching the same lessons? Among all the choices, how do

the demands on the students—the number of instructions to be remembered, for example— differ?

3. What prerequisites are necessary for mastering the skill being taught? Teachers must not assume that all learners have a common familiarity with the materials, language, concepts, or cognitive strategies involved.

4. Do the teaching materials have a motivating quality about them? Teachers should try to develop programs that are intrinsically appealing to students, as well as relevant.

195

More powerful programs mean increased mental work and potential technostress. This places greater responsibility on teachers to guide students in judicious use of computers. Teachers must consciously plan the structure of the computer-learning environment. If they succeed, they can positively influence the cognitive and emotional makeup of the student.

If we accept as a minimum objective the development of cognitive flexibility and creative use of information, then we need to design strategies to accomplish this. There are several areas where teachers should direct their efforts. Like their managerial counterparts in the workplace, they need to encourage open discussion about computers and their impact. Students must be sensitized to the risks of computer use. Since computers have the potential to alter the way people think and behave, students should be made aware of technostress and its causes. Teachers can do this by exploring with a group of students the differences between doing exercises from a book, for example, and learning on a computer.

Children tend to find such discussions stimulating and enjoyable, and they will begin to understand that computers affect thinking differently than do books or teachers. Comparative exercises such as this also help students realize that they can consciously shift their thinking styles in and out of each learning medium. They know, intuitively, that if they sit down to write a poem with the same mindset as when they sit down to play an educational computer game, they will be frustrated, but they are not accustomed to thinking about this.

Teachers must be careful to lead discussions in a non-judgmental fashion. For example, it is important that discussions not be reduced to the pros and cons of computers versus books. Discussions should be open to all points of view, encouraging children to speak their minds without fear of making a "wrong" answer. In this case, the teacher should listen closely to what the children have to say, because there are no wrong answers when feelings or responses are described. If teachers speak honestly about their own early difficulties with computers, or perhaps describe some other challenge that they had to face, students will be more likely to disclose their own doubts and fears. It is often necessary to draw children out in this way, because already many of them believe that their difficulties with computer education indicate a lack of intelligence. This is particularly stressful for children who are accustomed to being at the top of the class.

Discussion of differences in the way children respond to computers can lead to discussion of technostress. Role-playing here can be helpful. Teachers can demonstrate the characteristics of the technoanxious or technocentered person; a sense of humor here can help lower the defenses that the students may have in talking about the subject. Ideally, these discussions can become rich learning experiences where students learn to think about their feelings toward computers in particular, and, more important, toward learning new activities in general.

In talking about technostress, teachers might observe that students often find it difficult to keep track of time and to know when to leave the computer. Students could then be asked to pay attention to experiential signs that indicate impending exhaustion. Students need to build an "observing ego" that will monitor their mental state when they do computer work. Those students who already show preliminary symptoms of being technocentered are apt to be overly serious, deny that the computer has any effect on them, and think the entire discussion is irrelevant. It is a waste of time, they might say; they would rather work on a program. Helping these students take different perspectives, share their feelings about subjects of interest, and work with others in a close-knit group will all have a positive effect. These students will at first, of course, feel frustrated and resentful; they are probably accustomed to thinking of themselves as unusually successful individuals, not as candidates for help. They should be told that, while discussing these subjects may seem frustrating, the development of flexibility is a new challenge to meet.

197

One popular use of computers in the upper grades is in computer simulations. Science teachers in particular use simulations to bring to the classroom or laboratory unusual situations and environments such as space travel or underwater ecology that would otherwise be inaccessible to students. Running simulations can elicit numerous questions without risking the consequences of real-world mistakes. For most students, simulations are entertaining and thus motivating.

Simulations have their limitations, however, and it is important that these are explained. No system is so simple that it can be modeled exactly. A simulation of a pond cannot include all the forces and effects that act on that complex environment. Moreover, students become so absorbed in simulations that they easily fail to notice the built-in biases of the program's designer, and may overlook the importance of theory. They become interested only in the practical effects of their hypothetical actions. This reduced attention to theory, in turn, can undercut a student's ability to offer alternative views to account for phenomena that are being modeled. It also lessens appreciation for the fact that ultimately a model is a reflection of what a person believes to be true about the world and that there are many versions of the truth that claim to account for the same phenomena.

Placing inordinate trust in a computer simulation does not lead directly to technostress, of course. But turning away from personal observation and relinquishing our critical perceptions can undercut an appreciation of the complexity of the real world while placing the computer in a position of infallibility. This sets the stage for a techno-centered view of the world. Teaching strategies need to take the computer's limitations into account; simulations should not be allowed to replace real field trips or preclude class discussion of different views of the process under scrutiny. It is essential that students gain a sense of humility in the face of an extremely complex and wondrous physical environment. The most successful anthropologists, biologists, and other scientists retain this sense of respect and awe for the real world. They do not dismiss unquantifiable human values and assume that everything can be measured and manipulated. Children who place too much faith in computer models as paradigms of the real world risk closing themselves off to these intangibles.

Teachers should also discuss the cultural and social implications of computer use with their students. The general observation that boys have an easier time with technology than girls should be brought out into the open. Children know that girls are expected to play with dolls and that boys are expected to take an interest in mechanical things. By talking about this with students, teachers can help them recognize the influence of cultural norms on the way they learn. Teachers can encourage children to appreciate the reasons for different learning rates. This can help girls feel less out of place, more challenged, and better able to deal with any learning inhibitions they have. Boys should be encouraged to help out girls who are hanging back because they "don't like mechanical things." Dealing with gender differences in this context can set the groundwork for a later awareness of cultural differences

198

between men and women and can prepare children to work together as adults.

One danger that is already cropping up in computerized classrooms is the perpetuation of class differences. In classrooms where children are regarded as college-bound, teachers present computers as a technology to experiment with, a new addition to a child's learning experience. These students may already have computers in the home, a facility with technical vocabulary, and a vision of the extent to which computers can be useful in the working world. In schools attended primarily by children from working-class backgrounds and where college is not the assumed goal, teachers too often introduce computers as teaching aids only, an attractively colorful and entertainment-oriented substitute for a person standing in front of a class leading students in drill-and-recall exercises. Also, working-class students are often channeled toward using computers on a more basic level. Teachers may assume that if these students have a future with computers at all, it is as data processors, not as more creative professionals such as game designers, software writers, or systems analysts. Teachers need to encourage working-class children to think about computers in more open-ended ways. This should not take the form of sending children to a counselor to be told that there is good money in computer programming.

The influence of class factors on computer learning takes place on a fundamental level. Most educational programs are written for a middle-class audience. For working-class students, this creates a mismatch between school and the real world, a mismatch that is worsened when computer-aided instruction is used. A teacher can make allowances for a student's background, providing correctives or helping the student perceive problems in a new way. Computer programs don't make such allowances. Teachers need to be sensitive to cultural influences, despite the fact that they themselves, like others, have

199

been trained to think of society as a classless melting pot. Ignoring reality lets this two-track system continue.

A useful tool for the computer teacher is the small-group exercise. Children need to learn to work together as a creative unit, which can serve as an antidote to the isolating effect of computer work. To demonstrate to students the value of this experience, teachers can use the metaphor of building a barn. Early settlers in this country rarely built barns by themselves. They invited the neighbors over to help out, with the unspoken assumption that the favor would be returned. The cooperation among neighbors allowed a solid, functional, and relatively complex building to be constructed. By working together out of necessity, settlers erected buildings whose quality often went beyond the dictates of necessity.

As an exercise, a teacher might suggest a problem for the group to work on together. Following the pond simulation, for example, the students might be asked to control the effect of acid rain on a body of water. This is, of course, an extremely complex problem that even experts are unable to solve. Students can then see that the complexity of the problem requires cooperation. They soon realize they will have to listen carefully to one another, each paying close attention to the complete message that the other gives—whether a suggestion is made with confidence or timidity, for example. The teacher can help students understand the importance of a reflective style of listening. To cooperate fully, students need to be able to grasp what others are saying well enough to be able to restate it in other ways and either build on it or suggest different approaches. This may take the form of "what I hear you saying is . . ." and "I see it differently and would like to talk about it." This prepares the student to separate the unchanging, objective problem being faced and contribute fluid, subjective, personal thoughts and feelings about the problem. Teachers should encourage students to use "I" statements when expressing their views about a prob-

200

lem. This reduces the tendency toward disembodied communicating.

Learning to take the role of the other is an essential aspect of working together in a small group. It shows children that others are listening to what they have to say. This draws students together as they simultaneously exchange ideas and learn about each other. They are impressed with the notion that the way each of us approaches a problem is personal to us.

To maintain flexibility in the group, the teacher should be able to identify different problem-solving styles that the children use. This may take the form of pointing out that Jon thinks the solution to the acid rain problem is a political one, while Alice views it as a technological one. The group should discuss explicitly the varying approaches that can be used to solve the same problem. This helps students appreciate differences among themselves and creates a psychologically safe means with which to challenge others on their views. All too often, adults shy away from drawing attention to differences we may have with others, or dismiss views different from our own. This often stems from an ingrained sense that expressing differences will provoke reprisal or rejection from those with whom we differ, a feeling that we unconsciously learn at a young age. Unquestioning respect for the authority of the parent and later the authority of the teacher is a prelude to unquestioning respect for the authority of the computer model. Children must learn as early as possible to be able to accept and synthesize differing views and styles.

Teachers, as discussion leaders, should be role models for the group. They should try to be genuinely respectful of feelings, interested in differing viewpoints, and aware of how personal and complex the process of problem-solving really is. Teachers must pay attention to the reasons underlying students' individual approaches: "Why do you think the way you do?" "What makes you choose that way to proceed?" Everyone in a group has a unique history that affects the way he or she views a problem. There is a tremendous reservoir of personal experience that remains to be explored. The search for meaning makes for a far richer experience than questions based on the search for data alone. It prepares children for a life of reflective questioning.

Reflection takes time, and teachers should not force students to contribute to the group. Allowing students to sit quietly and turn over ideas in their minds is extremely important. In silence can come profound insight. When a person is not forced to work on a problem, solutions can suddenly come to mind unexpectedly. It is common knowledge that scientists come to many of their most profound realizations when they are engaged in relaxed, "irrelevant" activities.

After leading group discussions, teachers need to devise learning strategies for individual students. This may not be the most "efficient" way to teach—compared to a coin-operated robot teacher, for example—but meaningful education must allow for each child's own character and personal experience. Teachers can suggest that students keep diaries where they can record their thoughts about learning to use computers: thoughts about the subject matter, feelings about what is being learned, suggestions of how they might teach the subject themselves. This exercise would make students reflect on their classroom experiences. Rather than concentrating only on educational goals set by the teacher, students would be encouraged to heed their perceptions of the learning process.

A teacher can help students appreciate the importance of inner experience by recommending the biographies of people who have been creative in their fields. These often provide wonderful portraits of the human aspects of discovery and a potent alternative to the computer-oriented model of achievement. Reading many of these biographies, one is struck by the dissimilarity between the computer model and the thought processes of great thinkers. The latter often take breathtaking leaps from everyday observations and centuries of theory,

202

reordering data in a revolutionary way. Darwin, for instance, observed many of the same phenomena that his contemporaries had; unable to reconcile old theories, however, with his unique perceptions, he proposed the theory of evolution. Many creative people are late bloomers (the worst epithet of the computer era). Einstein is a famous example of this: the genius who arrived at the theory of relativity was a slow starter at school who had trouble performing rote learning exercises. The thread running through so many biographies of creative thinkers is an awareness of what may be missing in conventional theories of the world, a willingness to break the rules and reformulate them. This requires an entirely different mindset from one attuned to the logic of the computer. Studying the lives of great innovators gives children insights into the struggles, choices, and uncertainties faced by a creative person. It also makes clear the great emotional commitment that capable men and women bring to their work. Too often, children disdain history as a collection of museum pieces rather than a source of models for behavior. Viewing the elegant symmetry of the periodic table of chemical elements, students may not be aware of the false starts and altered perceptions that little by little brought its relationships to light; they see only a neat arrangement of symbols, passed on to them whole.

Finally, teachers should structure their students' days to prevent overlong sessions at computer terminals and to include time for physical exercise. If students want to use the computers after school, a break is advisable between the end of school and a return to the computer room. This counteracts the effects of too many hours at a computer screen and provides a healthy change of activity, thus reducing the potential for technostress.

As guides and role models, teachers can affect a child's development significantly, but parents can exert a much more powerful influence. For this reason, parents have the most direct responsibility for protecting their children from technostress. Learning to guard against technostress is as important as reading Dr. Spock. Child-care manuals are, however, not particularly helpful to parents seeking to understand the problem of technostress in children. The recent emphasis on "natural" methods of child rearing also does not provide appropriate guidance for parents who must cope with the complexities of raising a child in an increasingly electronic culture. A parent's instincts are always crucial in determining the atmosphere and activities within the home, but to minimize the potential for technostress the parent must first understand the computerized world to which the child is being acclimated.

Merely lecturing children on the dangers of techno-stress is unlikely to do much good. The key task for parents is to identify the positive ideas and activities that can serve to dim the allure of a computer-centered view of the world. This task is an integral part of a larger goal: to encourage ideas and activities that support the full developmental and psychological integration of the child. The ways to accomplish this larger goal have been hotly debated by a plethora of experts for many years. Almost everyone has a theory as to what is important to the well-being of a child. An understanding of technostress focuses attention on a number of concrete, constructive actions that parents can take to help their children cope with the computer world in a balanced way.

First, parents need to devote "quality time" to their children. Quality time means several things: focusing attention directly on the child, being fully present (not thinking about work or bills or schedules), and taking pleasure in the pleasures of the child. This is difficult for many adults to do; in fact, it is ironic that something so ostensibly simple can be so difficult. Being fully present often precludes using technology as a medium of interaction. Watching television with one's children, taking them to the movies, or engaging them in video games can be enjoyable activities, but an over-reliance on these does not promote intimacy. It is important for parents to also get to know their children in a relaxed way, where there are no objectives or performance standards. Sitting together, walking, talking together are activities that cannot be improved upon. They help a child feel loved and wanted. Undistracted and undemanding parental attention reduces a child's feelings of isolation and loneliness, feelings which often make children—and adults—seek refuge in the satisfactions of intense computer involvement.

Consider a typical family meal. Most family members do not actually communicate with one another at dinnertime. They more often resemble a group of strangers who meet for a brief period, exchange fragmented comments, and rush on to the evening's separate activities. Because this sort of behavior is taken for granted, parents often do not realize that a child who is not sharing in dinner-table conversation may actually be suffering from technostress. Only a concerted effort can break this pattern of isolation. Parents need to slow things down. They should consciously try to talk and listen to their children more during meals, and spend more time with them after dinner. Simply improving the quality of these family conversations would give children a psychological boost.

Quality time means that we make physical contact with our children. Touch communicates warmth and acceptance. Without physical contact, we can become depressed or withdrawn. Sometimes we increase our work involvement to compensate. How many of us can recall those "touching" moments when, as children, we had a parent all to ourselves who lavished emotional and physical attention on us? Without touching, children may develop an aversion to physical contact as adults and, more broadly, learn to place themselves at a distance from the world around them.

Quality time means recognizing a child's emotions. Parents should make an effort to notice what children are feeling at a particular moment and to show them that they notice. On the parents' part, this requires empathy and the ability to feel comfortable with a range of feelings. Parents need not always interpret or analyze their children's feelings, but simply signal that it is safe for the children to express them.

Quality time also means playfulness. It means that parents are able to engage their children in a childlike way. Too many parents are weighed down by the world and are unable to share joy or spontaneity. They are capable of discussing problems with their children in a rational fashion, but they are unable to "lighten up" and indulge them. The result is a bond that is stiff and formal. The child learns that playfulness is childish and that childishness is something to avoid.

In addition to giving their children quality time, parents need to limit the time their children spend on computers. Parents who pride themselves on modernity find this difficult. They like the idea of trusting their children to know what's best for them. However, time limits should apply to both play and work on the computer. Parents find it easier to curtail the amount of time children spend playing frivolous video games; but inhibiting a child's creative work at the computer is difficult for most parents—it's overly reminiscent of interrupting a child's homework. But computer work is much more likely to lead to mental fatigue than is time spent on homework, and mental fatigue is a precondition for technostress. Once children understand how mental fatigue can disrupt a computer user's sense of limits, they will be more aware of when they are passing beyond those limits.

As in the classroom, domestic discussion of technostress is essential. Children should be encouraged regularly to discuss their feelings and motivations regarding computer use, as well as any progress or frustrations they are experiencing. Parents should point out that computer work is indeed work, although it may be voluntary and enjoyable, and that any form of work can wear out the worker. They can ask their children to watch for signs of fatigue, to notice those experiences that tell them to quit and move on to something else. If no answer is forthcoming, parents can then initiate discussion about such factors as distortion of time, increased errors, isolation, and other symptoms of technostress.

Drawing attention to increased errors is especially important. No matter how tired they are after long hours at the terminal, children will try to find and fix their mistakes while avoiding new ones. This only adds to their fatigue; the errors multiply, and frustration sets in, along with a sense of the child's imperfection in the presence of the computer's infallibility. Parents should urge children to take a break as soon as they find themselves in this situation. A clock (with or without alarm) located on or near the computer will help; children can then notice how long it takes them to become tired or error-prone, and also monitor the passage of time.

Parents need to watch for other signs of technostress in their children, such as chronic lateness for other activities because of involvement with the computer. Also, children may spend less time outdoors, and see their friends only if they work together on computer projects. Withdrawal from family conversations and a desire to be left alone are other indications of technostress. Parents should interpret these signs as a warning that more discussion is needed or that limits must be placed on their children's computer activities, as unenlightened as that may seem. Parents need to remind themselves that, "machine of the year" or not, the computer is no better a constant companion for their children than the television set. Children need a multitude of experiences if they are to develop well-integrated personalities.

Children always bridle at restrictions, but with computers the children's reactions can be drastic. A child scolded for playing baseball past dinnertime may feel frustrated or angry, but typically those feelings pass. As technostress sets in, however, children will harbor not only anger or frustration, but also a more deep-seated resentment. They may believe that the computer gives them a

207

special power over their parents, and refuse to obey parental instructions. They may claim that they are misunderstood, and insist that their rights are being violated. In their eyes, it is more than an activity that is interrupted; it is a very special relationship to the computer that is threatened.

Parents must hold fast to their insistence on limits; they must not be intimidated by their children's computer literacy. If the parents do have an appreciation for the usefulness of computers, it should not be permitted to weaken their resolve to forcibly draw the line when they suspect overtime at the terminal. For a child, learning to live with limits can be applied to many areas of life. As part of the socialization process, accepting moderation when using computers helps a child prepare for a balanced future (especially if that future is to involve computer work).

Difficulty in shifting contexts from computers to people is a key element of technostress, and parents should pay attention to easing these shifts. Transitions are a normal part of daily life. If we are reading a newspaper or working in a garden and dinner is announced, we tend to take a few minutes to wash our hands or otherwise get ready before convening at the dinner table. After a meal, there is another transition period when we help clean up or do dishes before heading off toward the evening's activities. Each of us has a personal sense about what transitions we feel are appropriate. The computer has necessitated that we plan our transitions consciously. Without this, we may be unable to make the mental shift from computer activity to social interaction.

Just as managers should encourage employees to stop computer work before the end of the day, so too should parents insist that children turn off the computer, say, twenty minutes before dinner. This allows the child to prepare for a situation requiring a different mental set and presence. It is also helpful if children vary their activities, alternating between computer time, outdoor play, and conversing or reading. Habitual change of context is impor-

208

tant for children because they learn that they retain the thread of the work left at the computer—especially after they get accustomed to the shifts—and that, in fact, varying their activities can help them work more creatively. Adults can suggest that children jot unfinished thoughts down in a diary or type them into the computer and save them for later. The short-term memories of many children are filled with scattered thoughts about problems they are trying to solve. Guarding these memories, or trying to, is a barrier to relaxed conversation or play. Like adults, children in this situation bristle at interruption and appear uncommunicative. A parent who understands this difficulty and helps ease the child out of it through transitional planning will have bridged part of the gap between parent and child.

All efforts to help children adapt to computers in a healthy way are well spent. They guide children toward a balanced relationship to technology in adulthood. It is unwise to assume, as many people do, that because parents were not raised with computers or because they have little understanding of how computers work, they should feel incapable of instructing their computer-literate children. What is required is an honest exchange of ideas between generations. Parents still need to look after their children with as much sensitivity, knowledge, and patience as always. Children, in turn, can heed the wisdom of their elders while sharing their own new experiences. This communication must be a truly cooperative effort.

# TEN

## Salvaging Souls

"These are the hardest patients to treat. The more insights you provide the more they agree that it's just more 'useful information.'"

*Anne*
Psychotherapist

THE PSYCHOLOGIST'S ROLE in treating and prevent-
ing technostress is one of emerging importance. Whereas
in postfigurative societies individuals looked to their elders
for role models, today it is often the psychotherapist who
is looked to for guidance. In technostress, as in many psychological disorders, therapy can help the victim clarify
and articulate the problem—and effect its solution. However, most technostress sufferers are able only vaguely to
articulate what is wrong, and therapists must tune in to
new circumstances and symptoms. Psychotherapists must
be prepared to reeducate themselves and to expand their
knowledge base because technostress as a psychological
problem has never been addressed before. The refinement
of treatment strategies will require years of study and
experimentation. It would be premature to outline here
specific prescriptions for curing technostress; the best that
psychotherapists can do at present is pay close attention
to those areas of human experience that are most closely
related to the pressures of computer use.

It is often an arduous task for psychologists to
change their thinking once they have established their
professional styles. Professional responsibility, however,
requires an openness to new discoveries. It is of the utmost
importance that therapists not view patients as closed systems, organisms isolated from the world. It is impossible
to understand the nature of technostress without taking
into account the social context of personal problems.
Trained to attend to the inner dynamics of their patients'

minds, therapists often overlook environmental factors. Consider, for example, the following case:

Sylvia, a VDT operator, lost her job because she consistently made too many errors. She went to an attorney and filed suit against her employer. She claimed that she felt pressured to perform beyond her capabilities, which made her emotionally upset and worsened the situation. She learned that she was eligible for compensation if she could prove that her difficulties were caused by working conditions, rather than her own psychological problems. The attorney sent Sylvia to a psychologist for evaluation.

Sylvia described her symptoms: burning eyes, nausea, headaches, irritation with family members. The psychologist began to ask about her emotional life and her childhood. He wanted to know what in her personality made her unable to cope with a high-performance information-processing job. The psychologist had been trained to recognize disease categories having to do with inner conflicts and defense mechanisms. Perhaps he was prepared to acknowledge that changes in patients' private lives—moonlighting, or marital problems—might aggravate their assumed personality defects. But he was unprepared to examine the possible effects of the workplace on Sylvia's mental state. He was unaware of recent studies suggesting that prolonged VDT use could lead to the symptoms Sylvia described. He seemed to have no idea of how work can affect one's brain processes. Nor did he know that a person's biorhythms—those natural inner rhythms such as heartbeat, respiration, and brain-wave patterns—are altered in electronic space. The psychologist diagnosed Sylvia's condition as a neurosis, ignoring the environmental factors that triggered her problems. Sylvia's compensation claim was denied, and the experience left her even more confused and despondent than before.

Psychotherapists must learn to recognize not only that the human psyche is heavily context-dependent, but also that the psyche cannot always be measured and defined according to Freudian criteria. Traditionally

213

trained psychotherapists are unequipped to recognize contradictions within a personality, for example. They have been taught to test for personality traits and to analyze emotions by placing them along one-dimensional spectra (from aggressive to passive, or from confident to insecure). They are accustomed to dealing with the effects of childhood experiences or, in a mechanical fashion, the conditioning effects of circumstance. These approaches can, of course, be beneficial to understanding a person's behavior. However, they are not complex enough to account for the attributes of technostress.

214

The overspecialized personality—especially the technocentered one—reveals a number of psychological contradictions. Technocentered individuals present themselves as being in command of their lives and able to make decisions freely. Yet in reality they are victims of compulsion, driven by their desire to conquer the technology, solving strings of problems until they are exhausted. Unaware of their plight, they lose the ability to arrive at creative solutions. They are autonomous only in fantasy.

They see themselves as powerful. They do not recognize limits to the problems they can solve; they welcome hard work and see no need for help from other people. They are unable to love, and even relatively simple emotional commitments, such as empathizing with another person or expressing care over a period of time, are beyond their ability. The simple becomes the complex. They are stunted by their condition.

Yet, their behavior seems extremely logical. At work, they exhibit a high level of comprehension and a strong desire for order. They can demonstrate reasons for everything they do and say—they are, after all, reasonable people. However, they reject completely the human dimension. They cannot articulate their own experiences and feelings, and they show almost no understanding of others' feelings about them; yet they are convinced that their obligations for human contact are fulfilled. They hear information, not ideas, feelings, or experiences. Their lives are broken up into component parts. While striving to behave logically, they are in fact distressingly difficult to deal with as human beings.

Finally, these unfortunates pride themselves on their flexibility. They can synthesize vast amounts of information at a moment's notice, and take pride in their ability to adapt to their superiors' requests. They dislike conflict, viewing it as nonproductive, and see themselves as willing to try anything to make a situation harmonious. This flexibility is imaginary. It is the flexibility of the "nonperson" who doesn't want to be touched by others but will maintain the minimum human contact necessary for peaceful coexistence.

215

Technocentered patients present a real challenge to the conventional psychotherapist. Hearing an interpretation of their situation, they assimilate it as "useful information" about themselves, but remain unaffected by it. They make a kind of pseudo-contribution to the session. They learn the rules of the therapy sessions and the proclivities of the therapist, and remain shut off to the possibility of genuine listening and sharing. When confronted with this, they may revert to comments such as, "Well, it's my training. I have to handle new information all the time. I learn what I can."

If psychotherapists are to succeed at all in reaching technocentered individuals, they must try new approaches. They need to pay particular attention to the patients' difficulty in expressing emotions. Emotions are threatening. Their existence—illogical, unquantifiable, and unpredictable—calls into question the patient's entire way of being. But they also provide an opening through which therapists can try to make contact. Patients who appear anxious, for example, are not completely closed to emotion. They know, consciously or subconsciously, that they have a problem. Anxiety may signal that they are vulnerable. For the technocentered individual, consciousness of anxiety is a first solid step toward an awareness of suffering and thus a knowledge of limits. In the short term, then, anxiety is not something therapists should seek to allay, as traditionally taught, but something to be drawn out and explored.

Recognizing the significance of emergent but unspoken needs is important if the psychotherapist is to help the technocentered person become more fully human. These needs also point to the deficiencies of electronic space. Psychotherapists generally think of a need as an inner state that motivates us to action. A need for affiliation, for example, moves us to seek out others. Unmet needs over a long period can have a deleterious effect on any organism. (The human infant deprived of love—touching, cooing, caressing—can suffer from a condition of emaciation called marasmus, from the Greek word for "wasting away.") However, a need can also be thought of in a deeper sense, as an expression of what is most essential to the quality of our lives. In a very real sense, needs define what make us human, and push us toward creating a future.

Needs are both socially and psychologically determined; satisfying hunger in Calcutta is fundamentally different from satisfying hunger in Los Angeles. But the very plasticity of our needs increases our potential for self-deception. Technocentered individuals block their recognition of the importance of specific needs, which heightens their sense of omnipotence. They see themselves as need-free, and everything in their work system serves to reinforce this illusion. In fact, only cognitive needs are met, and these only to the extent that they further the solving of work-related problems.

Technoanxious individuals, in contrast, present less of a problem; their emotions are still accessible, and they will acknowledge that their needs are not satisfied. Since they have not reached a dangerous level of technological overidentification, alleviation of their problems may be somewhat easier.

The psychotherapist has a responsibility to promote awareness of human needs within technostress victims. Of

216

all human needs, the primary one is the need to feel, physically and emotionally. Our need to experience the tactile world is akin to our need to express and share emotions. From our earliest experiences, both types of feeling help us build a sense of self. Emotions are an integral part of our nervous system and play a powerful role in our lives, even if we attempt to block them. It is essential to psychological well-being that we communicate what we feel. Arthur Janov, in *The Primal Scream*, has demonstrated clinically that at the root of neurosis is an inability to articulate feelings. His patients, by reliving traumatic childhood events—an agonizingly painful experience—improved when they learned to articulate their pain and became conscious of their shut-off mechanisms. In fact, the major developments in psychosomatic medicine since the 1950s have recognized the importance of emotional expression. Medical researchers have discovered that suppressed emotions often contribute to ulcers, high blood pressure, heart disease, and a host of other ailments. One study of terminal cancer patients in the mid-1960s even pointed to a correlation between cancer and unexpressed feelings of rage.

No feeling is more essential to human well-being than love. We can survive without love, but the quality of our survival is severely impoverished. When love is missing from our lives, we feel a painful emptiness and longing; to avoid this pain, some of us close off all emotional avenues. For love to thrive, and for us to thrive as human beings, we must be open to our own feelings and those of others. We must be, in a word, vulnerable.

Along with the need for emotional expression, we have a strong need to be productive. As psychoanalyst Erich Fromm has noted, we are an active and productive species by nature. We have a healthy need to contribute to our world, to shape it in accordance with our own nature, and to create alternative and rich ways of living. Fromm, however, is careful to point out that truly productive people are capable of cognitive flexibility, playful activity, and creativity.

There is empirical evidence to support his views. In a landmark study in the early 1960s by Donald MacKinnon of the University of California at Berkeley, one hundred twenty-five highly creative male research scientists, engineering students, and architects were given a number of personality tests to determine how they differed from their colleagues at large. The results showed that creative workers were the most productive workers. They were relatively unconcerned with small details—with facts as such—and more concerned with the meaning and implications of their work. Creativity also correlated with verbal skills and accuracy in communicating with others. Creative people, according to MacKinnon, had an unusual ability to "have readily available the experiences of their life histories." MacKinnon advocated that engineering education, which is usually dominated by technical concerns, be redesigned to include attention to the personality elements that he discovered.

One might assume that it would be a straightforward task for psychotherapists to help people come to terms with their needs, but this is not the case. Often therapists' own biases are an obstacle to patients' growth. Immersed in traditional, industrial-era psychology, most therapists have not grasped the essential changes of the electronic age.

Therapists usually fall into two traps when attempting to deal with overspecialized personalities in general and technocentered patients in particular. One pitfall is the reasonableness trap. This opens up when therapists find themselves in ready agreement with their patients, who present their situations as entirely reasonable ones. Patients might tell their therapists that a heightening of planning and control functions has reduced their flexibility. They need to spend a good deal of time alone in the evening so that they can relax from work and prepare for the next day. They no longer feel passion for their spouses;

the couples are more like friends trying to work out a mutually agreeable living arrangement. Besides, they're too tired from work to have any interest in sex.

The traditional therapist may allow most of these comments to pass because they all sound so reasonable. The problems fall within the range of normalcy that so many people have come to accept. There are no apparent difficult feelings, maladjustments, or great turmoil in the patient's life. The psychotherapist may conclude that it was probably the spouse or lover who pushed the person into therapy in the first place. The only obvious problem may seem to be a difficulty in making the transition from work to home.

Seduced by the patient's reasonableness, the therapist easily misses the big picture. By concentrating on details, the therapist leaves many of the patient's deeply buried feelings untouched. The patient's inability to distinguish between healthy needs and pathological ones remains intact.

The second snare that entangles many psychotherapists can be referred to as the process trap. This is more problematic for therapists because it requires that they reexamine basic assumptions. They invest years of time and effort in training, and to question its bases means questioning themselves as well. The process trap occurs when therapists view therapy sessions as forums for exchanging information. This dangerous trend toward communications theory within the field of psychotherapy is gaining influence. Gregory Bateson, a leading proponent, sees as central to psychotherapy the exploration of how messages between therapist and client are interpreted by each.

One wonders what happened to the richness of the therapeutic encounter. Psychotherapists now talk in terms of "functions," "messages," "codification," and "systems of communication." It is all too reminiscent of the "effective procedures" of electronic space. Fright and anxiety are downplayed; concern for messages replaces concern for emotions. Gone are the existential questions, the painful confrontations with the self. The objective of psychotherapy becomes correct thinking, "appropriate messages" based on "accurate perception."

When therapists take this approach with technocentered patients, they exacerbate the situation. The patients, without much anxiety, can join the therapist in an exchange of information—perhaps even a perfectly honest exchange. The cure is taken to be clarity of thinking. Many therapists refer to patients as "handling the process well," "doing good process work," or "improving their interpersonal processes." The patients can learn to improve their ability to communicate without fundamentally changing at all; in fact, their underlying condition can become even more obscured than before. When patients switch to therapists who do not take a communication-theory approach, the problems often persist. Patients have learned to take all the potentially profound experiences of therapy sessions and turn them into statements explaining why they "process experience" the way they do.

Communication-oriented psychotherapists feel most comfortable with technology-oriented patients. Herein lies the problem. Nothing is gained by partially altering a pathological condition, only to reinforce it at the roots; psychotherapy of this kind is an obstacle to change. At issue in a psychotherapy session is what it means to be fully alive. The struggle to obtain a sense of wholeness, a grasp of one's identity, and a development of rounded passions must grow into new experiences for the patient.

What is curative is not better communication, although this is undeniably important, but an encounter that leads to discovery of needs and a confrontation with the experiential truth of one's existence. Anything less than this will only limit the human potential of patient and therapist alike.

220

# Postscript

IN ORDER TO EFFECT a genuine computer revolution that will advance the species in a positive direction without sacrificing our most cherished values, all sectors of society must participate. We cannot—and should not—stem the tide, but we can insure that we are making careful and intelligent choices about its flow. It would be foolish to deny that computers *are* a fact of life for us all, and that they can indeed help us in many ways. No discussion of the effective introduction of computer technology is complete without touching on how we should go about choosing a computer system. It has been often repeated (and less often heeded) that the prime consideration for choosing a computer should be its purpose. Hardware and software should always suit a person, company, or family's particular needs. If a computer is to be used for small-business budgeting tasks, a system with a large memory capacity is inappropriate. Similarly, buying a software package to inventory the contents of our refrigerator is a waste of the technology.

As computer users, we should feel comfortable with the hardware and software of the computer system. For beginners, whether adults or children, it may be helpful to watch someone take a system apart. This awareness helps to demystify the computer, revealing it as the inanimate electrical appliance it really is.

Most definitions of computer literacy end with the user learning how to "drive" the computer. The drive model's message is: Switch on the machine and use the software. This is a woefully incomplete approach to computer literacy. We must develop a more critical view and watch for drawbacks and improvements in programs. Above all, we must be prepared to ask questions: Is the response time appropriate for the task at hand? Is there too much information displayed on the screen at once? Is there proper interactivity between the program and the support document? We must also be prepared to admit that for some tasks the computer is not much use at all.

222

The critical mind will try to discover the assumptions made by the designer of a software program. It will not be seduced by attractive colors, cute logos, or easy application. A program based on poor assumptions could be wonderfully easy to use—and inaccurate in its applications.

We must not lose track of the quality of our thinking. Software should be more than just a more efficient means to do what we did before; it should allow us to invent new alternatives to existing problems. With the introduction of new technology into an environment, habits and styles fixed by years of tradition are unfrozen. We have the opportunity to improve upon existing ways of doing things; we also risk making things worse. There is nothing inherently hazardous to our health about most new technologies. What is hazardous is abuse, misuse, and unhealthy adaptation to them. When computers enter the workplace, the school, or the home, they bring with them the potential for fresh approaches to old problems. It is our responsibility to seize this moment and make sure that the transition is carried out thoughtfully, with attention to the human side of the equation.

We have a long way to go before we fully exploit this opportune moment to our advantage. Because we believe the computer to be connected with progress, we don't spend enough time worrying about how computers should be introduced into an environment—only that they be introduced, one way or another, and as quickly as possible. We speak of the "race" to computerize before our competitors do; in the schools, districts vie to be the first to make computer courses compulsory or to find funding for kindergarten computers. Savings banks scurry to install automatic teller machines, lest they be left in the unautomated dark ages.

This headlong rush is at the heart of the technostress problem. The United States has made fewer studies on the societal impact of the computer than have western European countries. In these countries, particularly West Germany and Sweden, government, industry, and universities cooperate to assess the effects of the technology in detailed and well-controlled studies. In the business world, the assumption in the United States, as always, is that the invisible hand of the marketplace rewards companies that implement the new technology correctly and punishes those that do not. We assume that the former will have happy, well-adjusted, and therefore productive employees, while the latter will be plagued with work stoppages. Faith in the "bottom line" as the measuring stick of all things is misplaced, however. It cannot take into account the cultural mutation that occurs as maladaptation to computers grows. Checks and balances no longer work when technostress is the rule.

223

Technostress has demonstrated in a dramatic way the impact made by the computer on our inner life. It indicates a crucial limit to how far we can push the Computer Revolution. It represents a failure to move beyond industrial models that we have grown so comfortable with, but that are so obviously limited in tapping human potential. Poor planning and neglect of psychological life on a broad scale present a real threat to the human personality.

The existence of technostress suggests the need to upgrade the quality of our most recent thinking. We must question our most prized assumptions about the computer phenomenon. We must ask ourselves what a genuine technological revolution would do, what is historically possible for us as individuals and as a nation, and how we can establish conditions for meeting the vital needs of the population.

We must transfer from machine-centered objectives

to person-centered objectives, which support the development of emotional life, the expansion of meaningful knowledge, and the building of creative work. The computer is one part of this process, not the totality of it. A humanistic approach is the key to positive growth, and all growth—personal, corporate, or national—depends on achieving goals through a balanced relationship with technology. This balance must be consciously safeguarded.

224

In the corporate environment, this transformation requires more than simply common sense; it takes careful, long-range planning and design. It is critical that we redesign our major institutions with as much sensitivity and foresight as possible. Managers, educators, politicians, and social critics so proclaimed long before the first consulting fee was ever paid, yet in the real world it is this kind of cautious advice that is generally overlooked. When it comes to the purchase and implementation of computers in particular, it is advice that is almost universally ignored.

Change is upon us, and we must all take collective responsibility in choosing constructive steps that we as a society must take. We must learn what computers can and cannot do, study how they are used and can be used in the future, question their impact, and develop appropriate strategies that allow high performance and personal well-being to coexist. Only through broad-based interest and participation can technostress be eliminated. Above all, we must get into the habit of trusting our perceptions. If people are complaining, we should pay attention. If people are anxious, we should investigate the source of their anxiety. We must resist the temptation to buy into the myths of the computer; instead, we need to make unhurried, critical, and imaginative evaluations of the computer environment.

If the four major groups that have a particularly potent role in this reevaluation—business and union leaders, teachers and educators, parents, and psychologists—take their responsibility seriously, there is much we can do to make the computer a benefactor and not a tyrant.

# Bibliography

Apper, M. H., and L. S. Goldberg. *Topics in Cognitive Develop-* 225
*ment.* New York: Plenum Press, 1977.

Argyle, M., et al. *Social Situations.* Cambridge: Cambridge
University Press, 1981.

Bank Street College of Education. Center for Children and Technology, Annual Report, 1981–1982.

Bateson, G. *Mind and Nature.* Toronto, Canada: Bantam Books,
1980.

Beatty, J. "Task-Evoked Pupillary Responses, Processing Load,
and the Structure of Processing Resources." *Psychological
Bulletin* 91, no. 2 (1982): 293–323.

Bernstein, B. "Social Class, Language and Socialization," in P.
P. Giglioli, *Language and Social Context.* Middlesex, England: Penguin Books, 1972.

Berry, J. *Human Ecology and Cognitive Style: Comparative
Studies in Cultural and Psychological Adaptation.* New
York: Sage Publications, 1976.

Bettelheim, B. "Joey, a 'Mechanical Boy.' " *Scientific American*
(April 1953): 116–127.

Bettelheim, B., and K. Zelan. *On Learning to Read: The Child's
Fascination with Meaning.* New York: Vintage Books, 1982.

Bluestone, B., and B. Harrison. *The Deindustrialization of
America.* New York: Basic Books, 1982.

Blythe, P. *Stress Disease: The Growing Plague.* New York: St.
Martin's Press, 1973.

Boddy, J. *Brain Systems and Psychological Concepts.* New
York: John Wiley and Sons, 1978.

Borg, G. "Subjective Aspects of Physical and Mental Work-load." *Ergonomics* 21, no. 3 (1978): 215–220.

Bowles, E. "Towards a Computer Curriculum for the Humanities." *Computer and the Humanities* 6 (1971): 35–38.

Bronowski, J. *A Sense of the Future.* Cambridge, Mass.: MIT Press, 1977.

Brooks, R. "Towards a Theory of the Cognitive Processes in Computer Programming." *International Journal of Man-Machine Studies* 9 (n.d.): 737–751.

Cakir, A., D. J. Hart, and T. F. M. Stewart. *Visual Display Terminals.* New York: John Wiley and Sons, 1980.

Campbell, D. "Perception as Substitute Trial and Error." *Psychological Review* 63, no. 5 (1956): 330–343.

Capra, F. *The Turning Point.* New York: Simon and Schuster, 1982.

Chiang, H., and A. Maslow. *The Healthy Personality.* New York: Van Nostrand Reinhold Co., 1977.

Coburn, P. *Computers in Education.* Reading, Mass.: Addison-Wesley Publishing Co., 1981.

Cofer, C. N. "Constructive Processes in Memory." *American Scientist* (September-October 1973): 539–543.

Cohen, A. *Two-Dimensional Man: An Essay on the Anthropology of Power and Symbolism in Complex Society.* Berkeley: University of California Press, 1974.

Cole, M. *Culture and Thought: A Psychological Introduction.* New York: John Wiley and Sons, 1978.

Cooley, M. *Architect or Bee.* Boston: South End Press, 1980.

_____. "Computer-Aided Design," in H. Rose, *Ideology of/in Natural Sciences.* New York: Penguin Books, 1976.

Coombs, M. *Computer Skills and the User Interface.* New York: Academic Press, 1981.

Cooper, C., and R. Payne. *Stress at Work.* Chichester, England: John Wiley and Sons, 1978.

Cooper, D. *Psychiatry and Anti-Psychiatry.* London: Paladin Books/Granada Publishing, 1970.

Cosden, M. A., H. C. Ellis, and D. M. Feeney. "Cognitive

Flexibility-Rigidity, Repetition Effects and Memory." *Journal of Research in Personality* 13 (1979): 386–395.

Covvey, N. *Computer Consciousness.* Reading, Mass.: Addison-Wesley Publishing Co., 1980.

_____. *Computer Choices.* Reading, Mass.: Addison-Wesley Publishing Co., 1982.

Cowen, E. "The Influence of Varying Degrees of Psychological Stress on Problem-Solving Rigidity." *Journal of Abnormal Social Psychology* 46 (1951): 165–176.

Cox, T. "Repetitive Work," in C. Cooper, *Current Concerns in Occupational Stress.* New York: John Wiley and Sons (1980): 23–39.

Davidson, M. J., and C. L. Cooper. "A Model of Occupational Stress." *Journal of Occupational Medicine* 23, no. 8, (August 1981): 564–574.

Davis, G. *Childhood and History in America.* New York: Psychohistory Press, 1976.

Deaken, J. *The Electronic Cottage.* New York: William Morrow and Co., 1982.

Deal, T. E., and A. A. Kennedy. *Corporate Cultures: The Rites and Rituals of Corporate Life.* Reading, Mass.: Addison-Wesley Publishing Co., 1982.

Dertouzos, M., and J. Moses. *The Computer Age: A Twenty-Year View.* Cambridge, Mass.: MIT Press, 1981.

Didday, R. *Home Computers: Questions and Answers.* Beaverton, Or.: dilithium Press, 1977.

Dimond, S. *Hemisphere Function in the Human Brain.* New York: John Wiley and Sons, 1974.

Donaldson, L. *Behaviorial Supervision.* Reading, Mass.: Addison-Wesley Publishing Co., 1980.

Dorf, R. *Computers and Man.* San Francisco: Boyd and Fraser, 1977.

Dreyfus, H. *What Computers Can't Do.* New York: Harper and Row, 1972.

Dubos, R. "Science and the Human Person," in C. Walton, *A Challenge to Individual Identity.* New York: IPLI Press, 1967.

227

Dutton, J., and W. Strachuck. *Computer Simulation of Human Behavior.* New York: John Wiley and Sons, 1971.

Eason, K. "Understanding the Naive Computer User." *Computer Journal* 19 (1980): 3–7.

Easton, S., J. Mills, and D. Winokur. *Equal to the Task: How Working Women are Managing in Corporate America.* New York: Seaview Books, 1982.

Eiseley, L. *The Invisible Pyramid.* New York: Charles Scribner's Sons, 1970.

Elkind, D. *The Hurried Child.* Reading, Mass.: Addison-Wesley Publishing Co., 1981.

Ellul, J. *The Technological Society.* New York: Alfred A. Knopf, 1964. (Paris: Librairie Armand Colin, 1954.)

———. *The Technological System.* New York: Continuum Publishing, 1980.

Erikson, E. H. *Toys and Reasons: Stages in the Ritualization of Experience.* New York: W. W. Norton and Co., 1977.

Finkelman, J. M., L. R. Zeitlin, R. A. Romoff, M. A. Friend, and L. S. Brown. "Cojoint Effect of Physical Stress and Noise Stress on Information Processing Performance and Cardiac Response." *Human Factors* 21, no. 1 (1979): 1–6.

Florman, S. *Blaming Technology.* New York: St. Martin's Press, 1981.

Forester, T., ed. *The Microelectronics Revolution.* Cambridge, Mass.: MIT Press, 1982.

Freud, S. *Civilization and Its Discontents.* New York: W. W. Norton and Co., 1961.

———. *Sexuality and the Psychology of Love.* New York: Collier Books, 1963.

Friedman, A., and M. C. Polson. "Hemispheres as Independent Response Systems: Limited-Capacity Processing and Cerebral Specialization." *Journal of Experimental Psychology: Human Perception and Performance* 7, no. 5 (1981): 1031–1058.

Fromm, E. *The Anatomy of Human Destructiveness.* New York: Holt, Rinehart, and Winston, 1973.

_____. *The Revolution of Hope: Toward a Humanized Technology.* New York: Harper and Row, 1968.

Gardner, H. *Art, Mind and Brain: A Cognitive Approach to Creativity.* New York: Basic Books, 1982.

Gaydasch, A. *Principles of EDP Management.* Reston, Va.: Reston Publishing Co., 1982.

Giddens, A. *Central Problems in Social Theory.* Berkeley: University of California Press, 1979.

Goffman, E. *The Presentation of Self in Everyday Life.* New York: Doubleday, 1969.

Gunnarsson, E., and O. Ostberg. "The Physical and Psychological Working Environment at a Terminal-Based Computer Storage and Retrieval System." Stockholm: Swedish National Board of Occupational Safety and Health, Dept. of Occupational Medicine, Report 35, 1971.

Hahn, M. *Development and Evolution of Brain Size: Behavioral Implications.* New York: Academic Press, 1979.

Hamilton, V. *Human Stress and Cognition: An Information-Processing Approach.* New York: John Wiley and Sons, 1979.

Harris, M. *Cultural Materialism.* New York: Random House, 1979.

Hartmann, H. *Ego Psychology and the Problem of Adaptation.* London: Imago Publishing Co., 1958.

Henry, J. *Pathways to Madness.* New York: Doubleday, 1973.

Hofstadter, D., and D. Dennet. *The Mind's I: Fantasies and Reflections on Self and Soul.* New York: Basic Books, 1982.

Holt, H. O., and F. L. Stevenson. "Human Performance Considerations in Complex Systems." *Science* 195, no. 18 (March 1977): 1205–1209.

Hoos, I. *Automation in the Office.* Washington, D.C.: Public Affairs Press, 1961.

Horowitz, M. *Stress Response Syndromes.* New York: Jason Aronson, 1976.

Hunt, M. *The Universe Within: A New Science Explores the Human Mind.* New York: Simon and Schuster, 1982.

Hunting, W., T. Laubli, and E. Grandjean. "Postural and Visual

Loads at VDT Workplaces: I. Constrained Postures." *Ergonomics* 24, no. 12 (1981): 917–931.

Janov, A. *The Primal Scream.* New York: G. P. Putnam's Sons, 1970.

Jaynes, J. *The Origin of Consciousness in the Breakdown of the Bicameral Mind.* Boston: Houghton Mifflin Co., 1976.

Johansson, G., et al. "Social, Psychological, and Neuroendocrine Stress Reactions in Highly Mechanized Work." *Ergonomics* 21, no. 21 (1978): 583–599.

———. *Stress Reactions in Computerized Administrative Work.* Stockholm: University of Stockholm, 1980.

Joseph, E. "Future Smart Systems." *Datamation* 24 (1978): 72–80.

Jourard, S. *Disclosing Man to Himself.* New York: Van Nostrand Reinhold Co., 1968.

Kahneman, D. *Attention and Effort.* Englewood Cliffs, N.J.: Prentice-Hall, 1973.

———. "Pupillometric Signs of Brain Activation Vary with Level of Cognitive Processing." *Science* 199, no. 17 (March 1978): 1216–1218.

Kail, R. V., Jr., and J. W. Hagen. *Perspectives on the Development of Memory and Cognition.* Hilldale, N.J.: Lawrence Erlbaum Assoc., 1977.

Kalsbeck, J. W. H. "Measurement of Mental Workload and of Acceptable Load: Possible Applications in Industry." *The International Journal of Production Research* 7, no. 1 (1968): 33–45.

Kantor, R. M. *The Change Masters.* New York: Simon and Schuster, 1983.

Karasek, R. "Job Demands, Job Decision Latitude, and Mental Strain: Implications for Job Re-Design." *Administrative Science Quarterly* 24 (1979): 285–308.

Kendig, I. "Studies in Perseveration: II. Determining Factors in the Development of Compulsive Activity." *The Journal of Psychology* 3, (n.d.): 221–246.

Klix, F. *Human and Artificial Intelligence.* Amsterdam: North Holland Publishing Co., 1979.

Knight, J. L., and G. Salvendy. "Effects of Task Feedback and Stringency of External Pacing on Mental Load and Work Performance." *Ergonomics* 24, no. 10 (1981): 757–764.

Kohn, M. L., and C. Schoder. "Occupational Experience and Psychological Functioning: An Assessment of Reciprocal Effects." *American Sociological Review* 38 (February 1973): 97–118.

Komali, J., C. Moodie, and G. Salvendy. "A Framework for Integrated Assembly Systems: Humans, Automation and Robots." *The International Journal of Production Research* 20, no. 4 (1982): 431–448.

Korman, A. *Industrial and Organizational Psychology.* Englewood Cliffs, N.J.: Prentice-Hall, 1971.

Kreithler, H. *Cognitive Orientation and Behavior.* New York: Springer Publishing Co., 1976.

Kuhn, T. *The Nature of Scientific Revolutions.* Chicago: University of Chicago Press, 1968.

Langer, S. K. *Mind: An Essay on Human Feeling,* Vol 2. Baltimore, Md.: Johns Hopkins University Press, 1972.

Lazarus, R. *Psychological Stress and the Coping Process.* New York: McGraw-Hill, 1966.

Lehman, D. *NATO Conference on Human-Evoked Potentials, Constance, Greece.* New York: Plenum Press, 1978.

Levi, L., ed. *Society, Stress and Disease.* Vol. 1, *The Psychosocial Environment and Psychosomatic Diseases.* London: Oxford University Press, 1971.

Luce, G. G. *Body Time.* New York: Bantam Books, 1971.

Luria, A. *Cognitive Development: Its Cultural and Social Foundations.* Cambridge, Mass.: Harvard University Press, 1976.

MacKay, C., and T. Cox. *Response to Stress; Occupational Aspects.* London: IPC and Technology Press, 1978.

Marcuse, H. *Eros and Civilization.* New York: Vintage Books, 1962.

———. *Five Lectures.* Boston: Beacon Press, 1970.

———. *One-Dimensional Man: Studies in the Ideology of Advanced Industrial Society.* Boston: Beacon Press, 1969.

Mead, M. *Culture and Commitment.* New York: Natural History Press/Doubleday, 1970.

Miller, J. *States of Mind.* New York: Pantheon Books, 1983.

Minsky, M., and S. Papert. *Artificial Intelligence.* Condon Lectures, Oregon State System of Higher Education, Oregon, 1973.

Mischell, W. *Personality and Assessment.* New York: John Wiley and Sons, 1968.

Mitroff, I. *The Subjective Side of Science.* Amsterdam: Elsevier Scientific Publishing Co., 1974.

Mitscherlich, A. *Society Without the Father.* New York: Free Press, 1970.

Montague, A. *Touching: The Human Significance of the Skin.* New York: Harper and Row, 1978.

Moos, R. *Human Adaptation.* Lexington, Mass.: D. C. Heath and Co., 1976.

Moray, N. "Where is Capacity Limited—A Survey and a Model." *Acta Psychologica* 27 (1967): 84–92.

Moray, N., ed. *Mental Workload: Its Theory and Measurement.* New Jersey: Plenum Press, 1979. (Stirling, Scotland: University of Stirling.)

Newell, A., and H. A. Simon. *Human Problem Solving.* Hillsdale, N.J.: Lawrence Erlbaum Assoc., 1972.

Norman, D., and D. Bobrow. "On Data-limited and Resource-limited Processes." *Cognitive Psychology* 7 (1975): 44–64.

Oborne, D. J. *Ergonomics at Work.* Chichester, England: John Wiley and Sons, 1982.

Ornstein, R. E. *On the Experience of Time.* Middlesex, England: Penguin Books, 1969.

Papert, S. *Mind Storms: Children, Computers, and Powerful Ideas.* New York: Basic Books, 1980.

Piaget, J. *The Origins of Intelligence in Children.* Translated by Margaret Cook. New York: International Universities Press, 1952.

_____. "Time Perception in Children," in *Voices of Time.* Edited by J. T. Fraser. New York: George Braziller, 1966.

Posner, M. "Cumulative Development of Attentional Theory." *American Psychologist* 37, no. 2 (February 1982): 168–179.

Pribram, K. H. "The Neurophysiology of Remembering." *Scientific American* (January 1969): 73–86.

Riegel, K. F. *Psychology Mon Amour.* Boston: Houghton Mifflin Co., 1978.

Rissler, A. "Stress Reactions at Work and After Work During a Period of Quantitative Overload." *Ergonomics* 20, no. 3 (1978): 13–16.

Roszak, T. *The Making of the Counter-Culture.* New York: Doubleday, 1969.

Rothenberg, A. *The Emerging Goddess: The Creative Process in Art, Science and Other Fields.* Chicago: University of Chicago Press, 1980.

Russell, P. *The Brain Book.* New York: Hawthorn Books/Dutton, 1979.

Sagan, C. *The Dragons of Eden.* New York: Random House, 1977.

Saito, M., and T. Tanaka. "Eyestrain in Inspection and Clerical Workers." *Ergonomics* 24, no. 3 (1981): 161–173.

Salvendy, G. "Human-Computer Communications with Special Reference to Technological Developments, Occupational Stress and Educational Needs." *Ergonomics* 25, no. 6 (1982): 435–447.

———. "Occupational Stress. A Significant Contribution to Effective Utilization of Technology." *International Journal of Production Research* 20, no. 3 (1982): 409–416.

Salvendy, G., and M. Smith. *Machine Pacing and Occupational Stress.* London: Taylor and Francis, 1981.

Sartre, J. P. *Search for a Method.* New York: Vintage Books, 1963.

Schank, R. C. *Reading and Understanding: Teaching from the Perspective of Artificial Intelligence.* Hillsdale, N.J.: Lawrence Erlbaum Assoc., 1982.

Schwartz, P., and J. Ogilvy. "The Emergent Paradigm: Changing Patterns of Thought and Belief." *Analytic Report Values*

233

*and Lifestyles Program*. Menlo Park, Calif.: Stanford Research International, April 1979.

Searle, J. "Minds, Brains, and Programs." *The Behavioral and Brain Sciences* 3 (1980): 417–457.

———. "The Myth of the Computer." *New York Review of Books*, 29 April 1982.

Selye, H. "Confusion and Controversy in the Stress Field." *Journal of Human Stress* (June 1975): 37–44.

———. *The Stress of Life*. New York: McGraw-Hill Book Co., 1956.

Shapiro, D. *Neurotic Styles*. New York: Basic Books, 1965.

Sharit, J., and G. Salvendy. "Occupational Stress: Review and Reappraisal." *Human Factors* (April 1982): 130–162.

Shye, S., and O. Elizor. "Worries about Deprivation of Job Reward Following Computerization." *Human Relations* 29 (1976): 63–71.

Sieghart, P. "The International Implications of the Development of Microelectronics." *The Information Society* 1, no. 1, (1981).

Simon, H. A., and K. Gilmartin. "A Simulation of Memory for Chess Positions." *Cognitive Psychology* 5 (1973): 29–46.

Sloman, A. *The Computer Revolution in Philosophy*. London: Harvester Press, 1978.

Smelser, N., and E. Erikson. *Themes of Work and Love in Adulthood*. Cambridge, Mass.: Harvard University Press, 1980.

Smith, J. M. *Evolution Now*. San Francisco: W. H. Freeman and Co., 1982.

Smith, M., B. Cohen, and L. Stammenjohn. "An Investigation of Health Complaints and Job Stress in Video Display Operations." *Human Factors* 23, no. 4 (1981): 387–400.

Smock, D. C. "The Influence of Psychological Stress on the Intolerance of Ambiguity." *Journal of Abnormal and Social Psychology* 50 (1955): 177–182.

Spear, N. E. *The Processing of Memories: Forgetting and Retention*. Hillsdale, N.J.: Lawrence Erlbaum Assoc., 1978.

Stammenjohn, L., et al. "Evaluation of Work Station Design

Factors in VDT Operations." *Human Factors* (August 1981): 402–410.

Stegler, G. "The Economics of Information." *The Journal of Political Economy* 59, no. 3 (June 1961): 213–224.

Sterling, T. "Humanizing Computerized Information Systems." *Science* 190 (1975): 1168–1172.

Strauss, G., ed. *Organizational Behavior, Research and Issues.* University of Wisconsin, Industrial Relations Research Association, 1974.

Sulloway, F. J. *Freud—Biologist of the Mind.* New York: Basic Books, 1983.

Sussman, G. J. *A Computer Model of Skill Acquisition.* New York: American Elsevier Publishing Co., 1980.

Toda, M. *Man, Robot, and Society: Models and Speculations.* Hingham, Mass.: Martinus Nijhoff Publishing, 1982.

Toffler, A. *The Third Wave.* New York: William Morrow and Co., 1980.

Waters, C. R. "Just When You Thought It Was Safe to Go Back in the Office." *Systems Management* (January 1983): 69–74.

Welford, A. T. "Mental Work-Load as a Function of Demand, Capacity, Strategy and Skill." *Ergonomics* 21, no. 3 (1978): 151–167.

Wertsch, J. V. "From Social Interaction to Higher Psychological Processes." *Human Development* 22, no. 1 (1979): 1–21.

Wiener, N. *The Human Use of Human Beings.* New York: Avon Books, 1950.

Wisner, A. "Organizational Stress, Cognitive Load, and Mental Suffering," in G. Salvendy and M. Smith, *Machine Pacing and Occupational Stress.* London: Taylor and Francis, 1981.

Zimbardo, P. "A Pirandellian Prison." *New York Times Sunday Magazine* (8 April 1973): 38–60.

Zisman, M. "Office Automation: Revolution or Evolution." *Sloan Management Review* (Spring 1978): 1–13.

Zuboff, S. "New Worlds of Computer-Mediated Work." *Harvard Business Review* (September-October 1980): 142–152.

Zwaga, H. J. G. "Psychophysiological Reactions to Mental Tasks: Effort or Stress?" *Ergonomics* 16, no. 1 (1973): 61–67.

235

# Index

Abbreviated language, appeal, 94
Adolescence, 134, 137–138, 158
Age, 32, 59
Aggression, 100
American Can Company, 62
American economy: elimination of jobs, 5–6, 19, 55–56, 63; foreign competition, 6, 60; generation of jobs, 6, 56; real income and credit, 59; two-class work force, 5; unemployment, 54, 56–59, 63
American Express Company, 44, 174
American Psychiatric Association, 119
Amherst College, 149
Anatomy of Human Destructiveness, The (Fromm), 84
Anderson, Ronald, 153
Androbot home robot, 148
Apple Bill, 149–150
Apple Computer, Inc., 7, 12, 63, 122, 150
Armacost, Sam, 7
Artificial intelligence (AI), 105, 106, 154, 162–163
Assembly line 29, 54, 56
Atari, 6, 148
Attention span, 145
Automation, 29, 54, 56

Bateson, Gregory, 219
Bell, Daniel, 57
Bettelheim, Bruno, 140, 164, 165, 166, 167

Biorhythms, 213
Blocker, Ann, 113
Blue Cross/Blue Shield, 38, 44
Bluestone, Barry, 58
Boguslaw, Robert, 30
Borg, Gunnor, 187
Boston Review, 147
Brain. See Thinking
Brazelton, T. Barry, 139
Bushnell, Nolan, 148
Byte magazine, 154

Carnegie-Mellon University, 51, 149
Center for Children and Technology, 158
Challenge, 89, 93, 95, 100
Character, 84–88
Chief Executive magazine, 174
Child development, 99, 147, 156–160
Children: non-adept computer users, 138–139; and physical games, 143–144; shifting contexts, 130–131, 133; social isolation, 128–129, 133, 136–137; socialization, 99, 123, 127; technocentered, 133, 137; technostress in, 125–130, 132, 134, 204–208; and technostress in parents, 139–140; video games and, 142–148. See also Child development
Citibank, 20
Clarkson College of Technology, 149
Class factors, and learning, 199–200

Clerical workers, 26–28, 31–32, 47; expectations of, 51–52, 176–177; and loss of control, 48–49; and pressure to produce, 41–42; self-perception of, 34–35, 37, 57, 65; women, 46

Cognitive psychology, 161–162

Compulsion, 93. *See also* Obsessive-compulsives

CompuServe, 112, 113

Computer-aided design (CAD), 40, 76

Computer-aided instruction (CAI), 152, 193, 194

Computer and Business Equipment Manufacturers Association, 33

Computer industry, 11–12, 42, 59–60, 114

Computer literacy, 89, 173, 221; for executives, 62; and job security, 5; and non-adeptness, 138–139; obsolescence of, 6; parents' encouragement of, 4, 134–136; for preschoolers, 157; schools and, 149–155

Computer monitoring, 44–45, 48, 64, 171, 181

Computer revolution, 2–25, 26, 223; advocates in, 3–4, 56, 154, 155; machine as model, 15; and technostress, 17–20. *See also* American economy; Computer technology

Computers, 221; and centralization, 40–41; cost of, 56; flexibility limits, 9, 12, 51; promotions for, 11–12, 114; in schools, 149–155; seductive features of, 6–7, 9, 14–15, 28–29; simple versus complex, 68–69; and thought, compared, 10–11, 14; user-friendly, 11–12. *See also* Home computers

Computer simulations, 197–198

Computer technology: adaptation to, 13–14, 17, 21–23, 54; effect on culture, 89, 157, 223; fear of 4, 8, 16, 20, 36, 138;

maladaptation, 88–89; overreliance on, 86–87; rejection of, 38

Computer widows, 109–110, 115

Conversation: as data transfer, 15; genuine, capacity for, 104, 106–107, 114; shop talk, 103; through computers, 51, 80, 112. *See also* Human relations

Cooley, Michael, 40

Corporate games, 69–72

Creativity, 76, 87, 147, 162, 218

Culture: and mental development, 156; transmission of, 123–124

*Culture and Commitment* (Mead), 123

Customized systems, 74

Deaken, Joseph, 11

*Deindustrialization of America, The* (Bluestone & Harrison), 58

Dialectical logic, 155

*Dragons of Eden, The* (Sagan), 11

Drexel University, 149

Easterbrook, Gregg, 113

Economy. *See* American economy

Education: computer literacy issue, 149–155; models, 160–161, 166–167; public school inequities, 152–153, 199; social aspects of schooling, 148; teaching versus understanding, 10; values, 193–194

*Educational Psychology*, 139

Efficiency studies, 29

Einstein, Albert, 10, 203

*Electronic Cottage, The* (Deaken), 11

Electronic romance, 112–113

Electronic space, 26–27

Electronic workplace, 39–40, 47–48; history of, 27–28; technostress in, 170–190. *See also* Management; Managers

ELIZA, 160
Elkind, David, 157–158
Ellul, Jacques, 23, 86
Emotions: evolution of, 10; expressing, 215, 217
Ergonomics, 186–187
Erikson, Erik, 134, 147
Errors, 181; children and, 146, 207; magnification of, 40; reading, 165–166; tolerance for, 131–132, 146
Everdell, William, 10
Executives, 62–63, 71, 174

Families, 103, 205–206
Fantasizing, 145–147
*Farewell to the Working Class* (Gorz), 56
Fatigue, 32, 33, 43. *See also* Health; Mental fatigue
"Flaming," 51
Freud, Sigmund, 93, 98–99, 147, 213
Friedman, Meyer, 22
Friends, versus acquaintances, 94
Fromm, Erich, 84, 98, 217
Frude, Neil, 114
Fujitsu Fanuc, 56

General Motors, 56, 60
Gorz, Andre, 56
Gould, Alan, 194
Grady, David, 125, 150

Harrison, Bennett, 58
*Harvard Magazine*, 125
Harvard University, 149
Harvey, Brian, 154
Hazardous working conditions, redefining, 31
Health, 32, 37; and age, 32; physical, 32, 33, 43; psychological, 84–85, 91, 98; visual ailments, 30–31, 33. *See also* Mental fatigue
Heart disease, 22
Henriques, Vico, 33
Home computers: family and, 128–129, 136; functions of, 7;

instructions for, 52; marriage and, 109. *See also* Computers
Hughes, Dave, 113
Human relations: of children, 123, 128–130, 133–134; commitment, 118–119; and development, 158–160; in electronic workplace, 45, 49–51, 80–81, 94, 179–180; empathy, 109–110, 116, 214; human needs and, 84, 86, 111, 216–217; love, 137; parent-child, 136–137, 139, 204–209; role reversals, 124–215; subtleties and ambiguities, 107. *See also* Conversation; Switching contexts
*Hurried Child, The* (Elkind), 157

IBM (International Business Machines), 11, 12, 45, 60, 70, 71, 172
Impulsive thinking, 143
Information pollution, 67
Instruction manuals, 7, 12, 52, 178
International Federation of Information Processing Workers, 31
Interpersonal relations. *See* Human relations
Interruptions, intolerance of, 41–42, 91, 93
*Intimate Machine, The* (Frude), 114

Janov, Arthur, 217
Japan, 10, 32, 56, 60
Jobs, Steven, 12, 122, 150
Job(s): challenge in, 172–173; competition for, 59; by computer, number of, 29, 55; mobility, 46; phased-out, 5–6, 19, 55–56, 63; redefined, 5–6, 38, 47–48, 172–173; rotation, 190; satisfaction, 8–9, 49, 78, 190; subdivided, 46; titles, 35
Jourard, Sidney, 119

239

Kaypro, 69
"Kids Can't Wait" program, 150
Koestler, Arthur, 87
Kohl, Herbert, 125

Labor, foreign, 6, 60. *See also*
    American economy
Learning, 175–176; and video
    games, 123
Lecht, Charles, 124
Levy, Steve, 113
Loftus, Elizabeth and Jeff, 142
Logan, Margaret, 147
LOGO, 154, 156
Los Alamos Scientific
    Laboratory, 20
Love, 137, 139, 217

McCarthy, John, 105
McCollough effect, 31
MacKinnon, Donald, 218
McLuhan, Marshall, 115
Maintenance Game, 69, 74–75
Management: and boundary
    problems, 188; company's best
    interests, 170–171; and
    computerization, 174–179,
    183–184, 186–189; and
    information flow, 181–182;
    middle, 174; and productivity,
    170–171, 174; worker
    well-being, 172–173, 182, 185
Managers, 49; and access to
    information, 64; assumptions
    by, 38–39, 72–73; computer
    monitoring by, 44–45, 48, 64,
    171, 181; and corporate games,
    69–72, 75; expectations of
    subordinates, 67, 73, 174–176,
    178; fears of, 56–57, 62–82;
    unemployment of, 63
Manufacturers: instruction
    manuals, 7, 12, 52, 178;
    support services, 39, 52
Marriage, 17–18, 103, 105, 109,
    110, 114–116
Massachusetts Institute of
    Technology, 86, 155, 156, 160
Mathematical logic, 154–157
Mead, Margaret, 115, 123, 124

*Megatrends* (Naisbitt), 82
Memory: computer, 11; human,
    15, 41–42, 95
Mental development, 154–156,
    159
Mental fatigue, 34, 42, 92, 132,
    196–197, 206–207
Mental processes. *See* Thinking
Miller, Alice, 137
Miller, George A., 151
*Mind at Play: The Psychology
    of Video Games* (Loftus), 142
*Mindstorms: Children,
    Computers, and Powerful
    Ideas* (Papert), 156
Morris, John M., 139
*Ms.* magazine, 112
Mumford, Lewis, 85

Naisbitt, John, 82
National Association of Working
    Women, 35
National Institute of
    Occupational Safety and
    Health (NIOSH), 26, 31, 32, 33
National Research Council, 33
National Science Foundation,
    152
Needs, human, 84, 86, 111,
    216–217
Networking, 112–113
Neurosis, 217
*New England Journal of
    Medicine*, 31
*New York Times*, 152, 153
9to5, 34, 190
Noise, sensitivity to, 30–31
Nussbaum, Karen, 35

Obsessive-compulsives, 95–98,
    108, 117
Occupation cervicobrachial
    syndrome, 32
*On Learning to Read*
    (Bettelheim), 164
*On the Experience of Time*
    (Ornstein), 130
Ornstein, Robert, 130
Osborne Computer Corporation,
    5

Papert, Seymour, 156–157, 159
Parents: attitude towards
    computer literacy, 4, 134–136;
    authority of, 99–100;
    relationship with children,
    136–137, 139, 204–209;
    technostress in, 139–140; and
    work ethic, 137
*Parents Magazine*, 157
*Personal Computing*, 125
Personality development, 98–99,
    134, 139
Personal space, 26
Piaget, Jean, 126–128, 156, 160
*Popular Computing*, 149, 150
Pribram, Karl, 11
*Primal Scream, The* (Janov),
    217
*Prisoners of Childhood* (Miller),
    137
Production, industrial model, 29,
    39
Productivity, 171, 174
Programming: costs of, 79;
    versus software packages,
    66–67, 79
Progress, concept of, 82
Psyche, 98–99, 213–214
*Psychology Today*, 51, 105
Psychosomatic ailments, 22
Psychotherapy, 108, 117, 184,
    185, 212–220

Radiation hazard, 33
Ransom Game, 69, 72
Reading: aesthetics of, 164;
    errors, 165–166; instruction,
    163–167; remedial, 152
*Reading and Understanding:*
    *Teaching from the*
    *Perspective of Artificial*
    *Intelligence* (Schank), 162–164
Reagan, Ronald, 4, 64
Relativity, theory of, 10
Repression, 99
Retraining, 58
Riegel, Klaus, 155
Robinson, James, III, 174
Rogers, Carl, 109
Romantic love, 102

Rosenman, Ray, 22

Sagan, Carl, 11
Sales, 50
Sandberg-Diment, Erik, 153
San Francisco *Chronicle*, 192
SATs, 152, 193
Schank, Roger, 162–163, 164–165
Schizophrenic children, 140
Schools. *See* Education;
    Teaching
Service Employees International
    Union (SEIU), 190
Service sector, 36, 50, 57
Sexual relations, 111–112, 219;
    networking, 112
Shifting contexts, 108, 109, 129,
    130, 133, 208–209
Silicon Valley, 6, 38, 77, 102, 117
Simon, Herbert, 154
Skinner, B. F., 160
Sloan-Kettering Cancer
    Institute, 20
Smith College, 149
Snyder, Thomas F., 151
Social isolation: of children,
    128–129, 133, 136–137; in the
    workplace, 49–51
Socialization, 99, 127, 158–159
Software packages, 12, 183;
    assessing, 194, 221, 222;
    trusting, 78; versus program
    design, 66–67, 79
"Sorsex" magazine, 113
Source, 113
Spock, Benjamin, 204
Stanford University, 105
Star Game, 69–70
Stark, Lawrence, 33
State legislation, 33, 150
Sturdivant, Patricia, 151
*Success* magazine, 148
Sweden, 33, 68, 187
Systems analyst, 71–72, 77, 90,
    91

Teaching: adaptation to
    technology, 192–198; data
    processing model for, 167;

Teaching *(continued)*
  prevention of technostress,
    192, 195–196, 202–204;
    reading, 163–167; software
    assessment, 194; teacher as
    model, 201–202, 203;
    teacher-pupil relationship,
    153–154, 166, 202; using small
    group exercises, 200–201; and
    video children, 145. *See also*
    Education
*Technics and Civilization*
  (Mumford), 85
Technoanxiety, symptoms, 16,
    18–19, 93
Technocentered people, 17, 18,
    82, 88, 92–98, 104; and
    therapy, 214, 218–220
*Technological Society, The*
  (Ellul), 86
*Technology Illustrated*, 113
*Technology Review*, 35, 64
Technostress, defined, 16
Teenage tycoons, 122
Television, 135, 144
Terkel, Studs, 44
Therapist, bias of, 218–220
Therapy. *See* Psychotherapy
Thinking: abstract, 159–160;
    brain and, 13–14, 161;
    computers compared to, 10–11,
    14; dialectical logic, 155;
    impulsive, 143; mathematical
    logic, 154–157; synthetic,
    154–155
*Third Wave, The* (Toffler), 8
Time: leisure, 7; for reflection,
    44, 130; sense of, 7, 43, 68, 90,
    93, 115, 126–130
*Time* magazine, 14, 124
Toda, M., 10
Toffler, Alvin, 8
Toys, 157
*Transparent Self, The*
  (Jourard), 119
Turn-key systems, 74

Unemployment, 54, 56–59, 63
Unions, 33, 189–190

University of California at
    Berkeley, 33, 194, 218
University of Kansas, 125
University of Minnesota, 153
University of Stockholm, 187
*USA Today*, 122
User-friendly, 11–12

Van Gelder, Lindsay, 112
VDT (video display terminal), 9;
    design standards, 33
"VDT" Risks Hotline, 34
Verbatim Corporation, 31
Video games, 123; educational,
    146, 148; effect on children,
    142–148
Visual ailments, 30–31, 33
Vygotsky, L. S., 159

*Wall Street Journal*, 151, 152
Warner Communications, 6
*Washington Monthly*, 113
Watt, Dan, 149
Weizenbaum, Joseph, 86, 155,
    160
Women, 46, 111
Woodside, William, 62
Work ethic, 98, 137
Workforce: two-class, 5;
    white-collar workers, 29, 34.
    *See also* Clerical workers
*Working* (Terkel), 44
Workplace: depersonalization in,
    49–50; electronic, 27–28, 39–40,
    47–48, 170–190; increased
    production, 30; working
    conditions, 31, 180, 183–184
Wozniak, Stephen, 12

Xerox, 15

Zelan, Karen, 164, 165, 166, 167